EARTH SCIENCE ACTIVITIES

Related titles of interest

Integrating Science and Language Arts: A Sourcebook for K–6 Teachers
Donna Gail Shaw and Claudia S. Dybdahl
ISBN: 0-205-16072-7

The New Sourcebook for Teaching Reasoning and Problem Solving in Elementary School
Stephen Krulik and Jesse A. Rudnick
ISBN: 0-205-14826-3

Cooperative Learning: Theory, Research, and Practice, Second Edition
Robert E. Slavin
ISBN: 0-205-15630-4

The Power of Problem Solving: Practical Ideas and Teaching Strategies for Any K–8 Subject Area
Juanita Sorenson, Lynn Buckmaster, Mary Kay Francis, and Karen Knauf
ISBN: 0-205-15943-5

Science in the Multicultural Classroom: A Guide to Teaching and Learning
Robertta H. Barba
ISBN: 0-205-15105-1

EARTH SCIENCE ACTIVITIES

A Guide to Effective Elementary School Science Teaching

Ira B. Kanis
Hunter College

Warren E. Yasso
Teachers College,
Columbia University

Allyn and Bacon

Boston   London   Toronto   Sydney   Tokyo   Singapore

This book is dedicated to Rose Blaustein, who, among many others, has led by example.

Library of Congress Cataloging-in-Publication Data
Kanis, Ira B.
    Earth science activities : a guide to effective elementary school
    science teaching / Ira B. Kanis & Warren E. Yasso.
        p.   cm. — (Science at a glance series ; bk. 1)
    Includes bibliographical references (p.   –) and index.
    ISBN 0-205-16644-X
    1. Earth sciences—Study and teaching (Elementary)   2. Earth
sciences—Study and teaching—Activity programs.   I. Yasso, Warren
E.   II. Title.   III. Series.
QE40.K36   1996
372.3´57—dc20   95-8376
                                                                CIP

Printed in the United States of America
10 9 8 7 6 5 4 3 2 1   99 98 97 96 95

Contents

Preface and acknowledgments

This book responds to the urgent need for a guide to effective elementary science teaching that presents a balanced integration of pedagogy, earth science content, and earth science activities across the elementary grade levels.

There are many effective ways to teach elementary school science. Two instructional philosophies seem to hold sway in contemporary elementary science education: constructivism and expertism. We have attempted to create a clearly defined framework of philosophy, strategy, method, and technique to guide preservice and inservice teachers, school building administrators, and curriculum developers in their efforts to increase student achievement in elementary school science. These philosophies, and the strategies, methods, and techniques derived from them, are described in Chapter 2 of this book.

The primary emphasis of this book is on new or revised earth science activities that promote concept development rather than mere verification of concepts learned by passive means. Classrooms where teachers use strategies ranging from student-centered to teacher-guided are ideal settings for the use of activities that help students to investigate science phenomena and events actively in order to construct concepts. The activities given in this book are designed to help students in such concept construction. More traditional teachers also will be able to use the activities included in this book effectively.

Student achievement can be measured in terms of improvement in students' problem-solving ability. By using activities in this book, students will gain an improved capacity to examine issues or events and to formulate a problem question that can be investigated. Their investigations will be based on a problem-solving procedure that is fundamental to all sciences but also is applicable to other curriculum areas and to life beyond the classroom. Problem solving is discussed in Chapter 3.

We have developed many science activities for use in textbooks, teacher publications, and city/state/national curriculum development projects. On the basis of these experiences, we have included earth science activities that employ ordinary kitchen materials and simple procedures that can be used effectively, in regular classrooms, by elementary school teachers who are not science specialists. Experienced elementary school science teachers also will find that the conceptual theme format and the new or revised activities provide a refreshing and unique approach to elementary school earth science study. Both types of teachers should benefit from the suggestions on application contained in Chapter 4.

In designing or redesigning activities for this book, we faced difficult choices as to which activities were most appropriate for inclusion in a thematic presentation of earth science concepts for elementary school students. In some cases, the choice was dictated by the knowledge that the earth science concepts in question were not cognitively appropriate for elementary school students. In other cases, simple activities found in existing science education textbooks could not be adapted for this book because they did not aid the understanding of concepts within a theme. Teachers are free to add their favorite activities to those provided in Chapters 5 through 14.

Chapter 15 provides a unique presentation of the development and use of authentic assessment procedures by classroom teachers. Also included are principles for developing new authentic assessment tasks that will meet the individual needs of elementary science classrooms.

This resource book is organized into chapters that provide the following:

- A clarification and reorganization of thought related to issues of teaching and learning in elementary school science
- An introduction to the five-step problem-solving procedure and how to implement it in the science classroom

- Graded activities that are grouped within the major themes of earth science
- A unique, comprehensive framework for using student investigations in authentic assessment procedures

Acknowledgments

We are indebted to our many colleagues in the education and science education community who, through their writing, speaking, and demonstration of teaching styles, have influenced the reconceptualization of the elementary science education philosophies, strategies, methods, and techniques presented in this book. We are indebted also to those who pioneered in the "hands-on, minds-on" approach to elementary science education and the introduction of earth science into K–12 curricula. Many generations of preservice and inservice teachers have helped to shape the ideas and activities presented in this book.

We gratefully acknowledge the support of families, colleagues, friends, and students during this intense writing experience. We also appreciate the efforts of Cormac Tully and Douglas E. Yasso, who turned our tables and activity sketches into esthetically pleasing text figures.

We are extremely pleased by the enthusiastic acceptance of the conceptualization of this book by Mylan Jaixen, representing Allyn and Bacon. The reviewers of the manuscript, Roseanne Fortner of Ohio State University, Joan Braunagel McShane of Jefferson Elementary School in Davenport, Iowa, and Betsy Mabry of Dewitt Waller Junior High School in Enid, Oklahoma, have contributed significantly to making this book more teacher- and student-friendly. We greatly appreciate the efforts of Nancy Forsyth, vice-president, Allyn and Bacon, who expedited the review, editorial, and production process.

part one

Pedagogical Considerations

chapter 1

Introduction

Why teach earth science in the elementary school?

Earth scientists may be the most important but least recognized people in our lives. They investigate weather phenomena such as hurricanes and tornadoes, large-scale earth movements that result in earthquakes and volcanoes, and changes in the earth's surface caused by such processes as stream and wave erosion. Also, they study how ocean currents help to moderate extremes in weather and climate, and they may descend into the deep ocean to study the longest mountain range on earth and its relation to movements of the continents.

Earth scientists study the evolution of living things and their surroundings. Another of their concerns is how our present environment is being affected by pollution of the atmosphere, land, and water.

The results of earth science studies help us live our daily lives in greater comfort and security. The weather forecasts on radio and television tell us how to dress for the day and give us storm advisories or flood warnings. Soon it may become possible to warn of impending earthquakes or volcanic eruptions. With such information, we all may hope to improve the quality of our daily lives.

Is there ever a time when we are not in contact with earth materials or natural phenomena? Is there ever a time when we are not attempting to make mental models that will allow us to interact better with these materials or phenomena?

From our own maturation process, we know that experiences with the natural environment allow us to construct conceptual ideas about earth materials and processes. Later experiences may cause us to redefine these concepts.

Early childhood experiences with natural materials, such as water and sand, provide a wealth of sensory (concrete) stimuli that help a child understand the world. As elementary school children's thought processes mature, they may apply such earth science understandings to explaining how the location of a town depends on characteristics of the physical environment such as water supply and amount of buildable land. Availability of food and of raw materials for housing, clothing, and types of transportation also depends on characteristics of the physical environment. Later, children use these concrete experiences

4

and conceptual frameworks to formulate and test mental models about earth science processes. Our concern with understanding and applying earth science knowledge continues into adult life and benefits from the early stimulation provided by teachers.

Teaching earth science through classroom activities

Most elementary school teachers have an unnecessarily limited view of the earth science topics that need to be covered in their curricula, syllabi, or programs. The only topics that are consistently covered are rocks and minerals, fossils, weather, and the sun and its family (the solar system). Themes relating to plate tectonics, earthquakes and volcanoes, the earth's interior, ocean water movement, changes in the land surface, and relation to environmental change are rarely given any consideration. It seems that teachers misperceive the difficulty of exploring such themes through appropriate elementary school activities. They may believe that the concepts are too difficult, that they can be explored only by using sophisticated equipment, or understood only through field and museum experiences. This book seeks to overcome all these fears and inhibitions by providing a series of classroom activities that explore the major themes of earth science using only easily obtained materials and simple procedures.

Administrators must recognize that teachers need time to gather and prepare materials for science classroom activities and time to trial-test activities in order to identify any potential cognitive and psychomotor difficulties for their students. We have provided the teacher with conceptual knowledge and stimulating activities needed for an effective, hands-on elementary earth science program across the elementary school grade levels. However, administrative support for all aspects of the elementary science program is crucial to its success.

All the activities presented in this book are designed for use in the classroom. Teachers who are fortunate enough to have access to natural history museums, science centers, nature centers, and national parks or seashores should make every effort to use such resources as a supplement to the activities presented in this book and to the regular classroom science program.

New York State was the pioneer in introducing aspects of earth science into the precollege curriculum in the late nineteenth century. At that time the course of study was called physical geography. Over the years, the purely geographical topics were subsumed within the social studies curriculum, and the purely geological topics were combined with solar system astronomy, meteorology, and environmental topics to form the modern earth science curriculum.

Even though earth science and the other sciences evolved as secondary science subjects, they have been selectively incorporated into the elementary curriculum because the topics are important to the daily lives of young students. In this book the term *theme* is used to describe a general statement about natural change or human-induced change taking place in or on the earth. For example, the theme for Chapter 10, "The constant motion of lithospheric plates causes folding, faulting, and mountain building," acknowledges the existence of lithospheric plates, their motion, and some of the consequences of this motion for the earth's rock layers and topography. The three graded activities included in Chapter 10 explore only a few of the concepts needed to understand plate motion and its consequences for the development of the continents and ocean basins over time.

We had to make choices about the inclusion of some concepts in the plate tectonic theme. The inclusion of a volcano activity might have led to exploring concepts about subduction of plates, magma generation, and fissure flows, or volcanoes, that result when magma reaches the surface. However, these concepts were considered to be too advanced for the grade 5–6 student. Even though volcano activities are included in many elementary science activity books, such activities are meaningless unless students first understand the physical processes that lead to volcano formation. Activities chosen for this book are only those that help to develop concepts that are functional for the students at the intended grade levels.

The relevance of this theme for Chapter 10 and the other themes in the book that deal with changes in and on the earth is supported by the major themes of elementary earth science found in both the New York State Education Department's *Elementary Science Syllabus* (1984) and the New York City Board of Education's *Essential Learning Outcomes: Science* (1989). In the latter document, the major earth science theme throughout the elementary grades is "The earth is in a constant state of change that can be observed and measured."

The choice of themes for this book that relate to physical changes on our planet is supported also by some of the conceptual themes listed as the basis for revision of earth science curriculum even in the years immediately preceding plate tectonic theory. Two such themes, found in the *Earth Science Curriculum Project,* are *universality of change* and *uniformitarianism: key to interpreting the past* (American Geological Institute, 1964). These themes have guided many elementary and secondary earth science reform efforts and are present in grade-appropriate themes in this book.

Key concepts explored through activities in this book are recommended in "Standard 4–Science" in Frameworks for Mathematics, Science and Technology (University of the State of New York, State Education Department, 1994). The concepts and behaviors ("outcomes") for elementary-level students, as specified in the Frameworks, relate to observation and description of natural events such as the earth–sun–moon relationship; atmosphere, hydrosphere, and lithosphere interactions; and the interrelationships between life forms and the earth's physical environment.

From their earliest years, children in earthquake-prone areas need to know how to survive major quakes that occur with little or no warning. Almost any location in the United States can be subject to strong thunderstorms and tornadoes. Therefore, all children should be aware of severe storm forecasts that give warnings of only minutes to hours before such events. Those living in areas prone to river flooding or coastal storm surges need to know how to acquire and process information on such hazards, which are predictable for many hours or even many days in advance.

Earth scientists are continually increasing their knowledge of earth processes and developing new instruments or techniques to investigate the behavior of the hidden earth, oceans, and the atmosphere. These developments have always resulted in change in school science curriculum. However, a major impetus for radical earth science curriculum innovation was the formulation of plate tectonic theory in 1968. This theory explored the origin and movement of the pieces of lithosphere that form the continents and ocean basins. Also, the theory explained why earthquakes and volcanoes occur in the circum-Pacific, Mediterranean, and Middle Eastern areas.

Overall, the development of plate tectonic theory allowed curriculum developers to integrate the earth science subjects, such as volcanoes, earthquakes, and ocean basin formation, which previously had been isolated units in the curriculum. The earth science themes chosen for inclusion in this book are derived from the results of such plate tectonic investigations, as well as from atmosphere and hydrosphere studies and the new emphasis on the interaction between humans and their environment.

The revolutionary development of earth science knowledge has not yet resulted in elementary curricula, syllabi, and programs that help children achieve the level of earth science literacy that is necessary for analyzing Science, Technology, and Society issues. Therefore, this book presents the conceptual themes of elementary school earth science that should result in children acquiring the knowledge, skills, and attitudes that will enable them to function as "science-literate" adults. Inclusion of these themes is supported by their being identified as some of the *benchmarks for scientific literacy* described by *Project 2061* of the American Association for the Advancement of Science (1993).

Themes chosen for inclusion in this book emphasize the fact that the child's environment is undergoing constant change and that children can comprehend and measure some of these changes. For example, Chapters 9 and 10 explore the themes of continent and ocean basin changes caused by plate tectonic motions and surface phenomena such as earthquakes, faulting, folding, and mountain building related to these motions.

chapter 2

The art of teaching elementary school science

Teaching philosophies and strategies: The constructivism and expertism dichotomy

Every day, elementary school teachers face a staggering variety of tasks. These range from nurturing and instructing each child, through managing the class as a whole, to participating in professional development activities. As a result, teachers find it difficult to think conceptually about the fourteen common branch subject areas.

Is there a philosophy of instruction that can be applied to all common branch subjects? Even if you cannot answer this general question, do *you* have such a philosophy, and do you employ strategies, methods, and techniques that are specific to individual subjects? Such questions may not seem relevant to your daily routine, yet the answers can mean the difference between student success and failure.

This book attempts to identify and categorize the answers to questions of philosophy, strategy, method, and technique that apply to the teaching of elementary school science. Of current interest are two opposing philosophies of science teaching: expertism and constructivism. *Expertism* is a new term coined to describe the philosophy wherein the teacher is the central player, the source of all knowledge, and children are merely empty vessels needing to be filled with science concepts and facts. According to this philosophy, children come to us as question marks and leave as periods. Their natural curiosity is squelched in favor of rote learning. In *constructivism,* the individual student is the central player: the source of all questions. According to this philosophy, children come to us as a variety of seedlings and leave as flowering plants. Their natural curiosity is nurtured, and rote learning is eliminated.

Strategies are the second level of organization in the pedagogical hierarchy shown in Figure 2-2. Strategies are carefully conceived plans for implementing a philosophy. Student-centered strategies are used to implement the philosophy of constructivism, whereas teacher-centered strategies are used to implement the philosophy of expertism. The advantages and disadvantages of these two contrasting science teaching strategies are diagrammed at the top and bottom of Figure 2-1. As can be seen in this listing of advantages and disadvantages, the student-centered strategy actively encourages students to participate in decisions about their learning but may limit inclusiveness of the curriculum and its logical development. In addition, teachers must employ interpersonal and management skills to promote individual student mastery of concepts. In contrast, the teacher-centered strategy has the advantage of allowing the curriculum to be covered in a logical sequence. Teachers' management skills are focused on group mastery of concepts as revealed by objective assessment procedures. However, the use of this strategy prevents students from becoming actively engaged in true discovery of science phenomena and relationships.

Science educators have long sought the ideal of the student-centered elementary school classroom. However, many elementary school teachers have used teacher-centered science instruction because they lacked the confidence and the staff development support necessary to implement more innovative teaching and learning strategies. Transitional steps toward the goal of a student-centered instructional strategy are represented by the upward sequence of modified teacher-centered, teacher-guided, and modified student-centered strategies listed in the left-hand column of Figure 2-1. Logical changes in the advantages and disadvantages of the contrasting strategies accompany each step in the transition.

Many teachers find comfort with an approach that lies between the extremes of student-centered and teacher-centered strategies. Because of extrinsic demands, it is difficult for teachers to give up control of instruction completely and become equal partners with their students in the learning process. A logical step toward that goal is *teacher-guided instruction*. A teacher-guided strategy allows the flexibility of choosing and adapting methods that will address the diverse needs and learning styles found in a typical elementary school science classroom.

The teacher-guided strategy is placed in a central position in the pedagogical sequence shown in Figure 2-2. A teacher-guided strategy might begin with the use of teacher-directed methods and then introduce teacher-guided methods as students demonstrated mastery of problem-solving (free inquiry) skills. In this way, the teacher can meet the demands of the curriculum and the schedule while still facilitating skills development.

Figure 2-1 lists the advantages and disadvantages of the five teaching strategies but does not explain the roles of the teacher and students and their interactions within each strategy. Those roles and interactions are as follows:

Student-centered strategy:

1. Students' interests determine science themes.
2. Student discussion identifies questions to be investigated.
3. Students design and conduct research and investigations.

STRATEGY	ADVANTAGES	DISADVANTAGES
Student-centered (concept construction)	Students are more highly motivated and self-directed (intrinsic reward). Students learn from one another. Emphasis is on process (learning how to learn) rather than product (fact learning). Pace of learning is based on individually demonstrated mastery of concepts.	Greater teacher time is required in planning for each group/individual. Equipment needs are diverse. Many important concepts may be unexplored. Logical curriculum sequence may be violated. High demand is placed on teacher's classroom management skills (equipment, evaluation, and grading).
Modified student-centered		
Teacher-guided		
Modified teacher-centered		
Teacher-centered (concept demonstration)	Economy of teacher planning time. Minimal equipment needs. All important science concepts can be covered. Logical curriculum sequence can be imposed. Low demand is made on teacher's classroom management skills (equipment, evaluation, and grading).	No allowance for individual differences. Little opportunity for student-to-student interaction. No concrete/manipulative experiences for students. High demand on teacher's skill to capture interest of the whole class. Emphasis is on product (factual learning) rather than on process (learning how to learn). Pace of learning is based on "class average" of mastery of concepts.

FIGURE 2-1.   ADVANTAGES AND DISADVANTAGES OF CONTRASTING SCIENCE TEACHING STRATEGIES

4. Students present findings and lead the class to formulate appropriate concepts or conclusions.
5. The teacher facilitates individual student or group activities and assures that misconceptions are eliminated.

Modified student-centered strategy:

1. The teacher presents science themes.
2. Student discussion identifies some of the questions to be investigated.
3. Teacher and students together, or groups of students, collaborate on the design of research and investigations.
4. Student presentations are used as a guide to formulating appropriate concepts and conclusions.
5. The teacher guides student activities to achieve thematic goals and objectives.
6. The teacher facilitates individual student or group activities and assures that misconceptions are eliminated.

Teacher-guided strategy:

1. State and district syllabi or curricula are used as a guide for themes and topics for study.
2. Student discussion identifies some of the questions to be investigated.
3. The teacher selects those student questions to be investigated and prescribes others.
4. The teacher provides a variety of research opportunities and investigations.
5. Students formulate appropriate concepts and conclusions.
6. The teacher dispels misconceptions and provides opportunities for application of the newly acquired concepts.

Modified teacher-centered strategy:

1. State and district syllabi or curricula prescribe themes and topics for study.
2. The teacher introduces questions that lead to convergent or divergent thinking.
3. Student investigations confirm concepts introduced by the teacher.
4. The teacher elicits summary statements of concepts and facts from students.

Teacher-centered strategy:

1. State and district syllabi or curricula prescribe themes and topics for study.
2. Student questions and discussion center around the teacher's lecture and demonstrations.
3. Students restate learned concepts and facts.

Teaching methods and techniques

Teaching methods are systematic plans for attaining the goals and objectives of the science curriculum. Methods are the third level of organization in the pedagogical hierarchy shown in Figure 2-2. The four basic teaching methods are as follows:

1. Cooperative learning
2. Contract learning
3. Use of learning centers
4. The teacher demonstration lesson

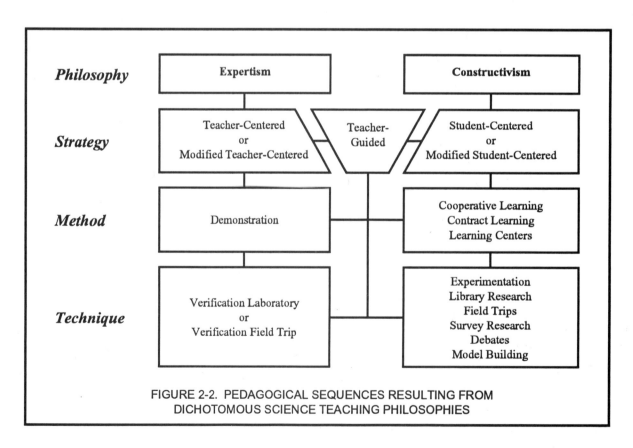

FIGURE 2-2. PEDAGOGICAL SEQUENCES RESULTING FROM
DICHOTOMOUS SCIENCE TEACHING PHILOSOPHIES

One or more of these methods may allow you to implement the teaching strategy you are employing. These methods are discussed next, and some of the techniques that are applicable to each are described.

Techniques, the fourth level of organization, are defined by the procedures (e.g., research, debate, laboratory) that individual students or student groups use in completing the science learning task.

The cooperative learning method

Grouping of students for hands-on learning or other suitable activities is called *cooperative learning.* It is a powerful method for achieving content learning, process skill development, and socialization.

Johnson and Johnson (1987) call for fundamental research in all aspects of the cooperative learning experience. On the basis of present knowledge, however, they believe that cooperative learning, "best suits problem solving, decision making and critical thinking."

Teachers of early childhood students may find that true cooperative learning is difficult to achieve. Young students can work in groups organized around a shared task that does not require higher level thinking skills. In early childhood, many of the students lack the social skills (e.g., sharing, taking turns, listening to others) necessary to work within a group that has as its objective using higher level thinking skills for the attainment of a common goal.

Modern educational practice suggests that groupings of students should be heterogeneous. Creating groups of four to six students aids classroom management and allows for equal student contribution by virtue of rotation of role assignments within each group. In particular, such groupings promote gender equity because, for example, girls do not end up acting solely as data recorders while boys manipulate the equipment. Weaker students, as they perform different roles, can make contributions to organization and idea flow that help the group attain its goals and objectives. In the process, students learn to value the opinions of others and to have rational discussions of alternative strategies for achieving the group's goals and objectives.

Groups report their findings to the class during scheduled discussion times at the end of a class period or unit of study. Discussion of group findings leads to the felicitous result of students learning from students. In this process, the teacher acts as a mentor.

Management tasks in the cooperative learning method

The teacher's task in establishing, managing, and mentoring cooperative learning is discussed by Johnson and Johnson (1986). Their identification of role specifics seems to reflect a teacher-centered or modified teacher-centered strategy. However, a more student-centered approach to cooperative learning can be used.

In cooperative learning there are five management tasks that are independent of the pedagogical strategy being employed:

1. Engage in decision making about academic and group goals or objectives, the size of student groups, student role assignment within groups, room arrangement, and the materials and procedures to be used. Johnson and Johnson (1986) define five general role assignments for each cooperative learning group, regardless of subject:
    a. Summarizer-checker
    b. Researcher-runner
    c. Recorder
    d. Encourager
    e. Observer

    We suggest a redefinition of the five roles to facilitate cooperative learning in elementary science classrooms:
    a. Materials handler
    b. Experimenter
    c. Recorder
    d. Reporter
    e. Researcher

    If groups include more than five individuals, roles can be shared, or students can perform multiple roles in smaller groups.
2. Focus on solving the problem. Students create an operational definition of the problem, perform their roles, and establish criteria for successful completion of the task.
3. Provide mentoring and facilitation by observing the functioning of each group and of the individuals within each group. If necessary, the teacher interacts with each group while it is working in order to improve group dynamics or the group's ability to achieve concept development. The interaction between teacher and groups, as well as within-group interaction, makes the cooperative learning method a powerful aid to learning.

4. Bring the cooperative learning process to closure. As part of closure, the teacher evaluates individual and group performance in achieving mastery of the task as each group reports its findings.
5. Encourage the entire class to generalize about the results and to achieve understanding of a new concept or new application of an existing concept. The teacher brings closure to the class effort by reviewing the important concepts and conclusions.

Techniques useful in cooperative learning

A variety of techniques can be used with the cooperative learning method. These include experimentation, library research, field trip and survey research, debates, and model building. These techniques are listed next and described as if they were to be used alone in a problem-solving situation. In many problem-solving activities, however, two or more techniques can usefully be combined.

EXPERIMENTATION   Experimentation is one of the best techniques for concept and skill development in science. It teaches students the need to define the problem carefully, state a working hypothesis, carry out an experimental procedure, and analyze its results.

LIBRARY RESEARCH   The library research technique makes use of all types of multimedia technology. The technique is useful in problem-solving situations where experimentation is impossible or is of limited value. Library research includes all the problem-solving steps used in experimentation, except that data gathering from the various media is substituted for laboratory experimentation.

FIELD TRIPS AND SURVEY RESEARCH   Science experiences should not be limited to the classroom. Outdoor environments provide many opportunities for problem-solving activities that will include either data gathering or experimentation. Such activities can be performed at school playgrounds, zooligical parks, museums, planetariums, nature centers, and aquariums.

Survey research gathers and uses public opinion to identify and solve problems.

DEBATES   A debate provides a platform for presenting oral arguments to support opposing views about issues of Science, Technology, and Society. Then the "audience" uses problem-solving skills to make a decision about a course of action to take to ameliorate the problem.

MODEL BUILDING   Building a physical model may be a means of solving Science, Technology, and Society problems. Such models could be charts, dioramas, mechanical constructions, or biological assemblages. Science concepts are used or discovered in the process of building models.

The contract method

Teachers and students who work together to identify learning objectives and plan for the fulfillment of those objectives are engaging in contract learning. The contract learning method is most often used with individual students to reinforce and support independent learning activities. The method is best employed with students who require a minimum of teacher guidance while they complete a series of tasks that lead to development of new concepts or provide reinforcement. The agreed-on tasks may require the use of a learning center plus one or more of the techniques already discussed under the cooperative learning method.

Upon completion of the contract, students submit documentation that demonstrates completion of the tasks. In addition, students may be obligated to present an oral report to the teacher or the class.

Management tasks in the contract learning method

The contract learning method presumes that a student-centered, modified student-centered, or teacher-guided strategy is being emphasized. Therefore, the management tasks include negotiation of all aspects of the contract, whether for individual enrichment or for reinforcement. The four principal management tasks are as follows:

1. Help the student clarify the problem and identify the learning objectives that will be the criteria for successful completion of the tasks specified in the contract. Also specified is a timeline for completion of the contract.
2. Provide necessary resources or give instruction on how the student can access such resources.
3. Provide mentoring for students. In contrast with teacher activities during cooperative learning, in contract learning mentoring should require only occasional interaction with students. The amount of teacher–student interaction will depend on the level of student experience with independent learning and on whether the contract has been designed for enrichment or reinforcement.

4. Bring closure. At completion of the contract or expiration of the time limit, the student submits documentation and may do an oral presentation to the teacher or to the entire class. As part of closure, the teacher evaluates or helps the student to evaluate how well the contract objectives have been met.

Techniques useful in the contract learning method

All techniques described in the section on cooperative learning can be used in contract learning. Another popular feature of contract learning is the learning center.

LEARNING CENTERS   A learning center is a portion of the classroom dedicated to facilitation of independent learning. Physically, it can be as simple as a table or bookshelf or as sophisticated as a laboratory bench with computer and audiovisual equipment. In any of its manifestations, it will contain all the materials needed to accomplish the learning tasks of one or two individuals at a time.

The learning center individualizes learning by permitting students to work at their own pace. It encourages them to construct concepts by exploring, discovering, and creating. The materials in the center will change and will be coordinated with each new unit of study. The learning stations may present new materials, review and reinforce previously learned concepts, or present opportunities for the application of newly mastered concepts.

The demonstration lesson method

Many elementary school teachers rely too often on lectures and teacher demonstrations in their attempts to transmit science concepts. Many teachers believe that they must use this method to cover all the material required to meet extrinsic criteria such as grade examinations, syllabi, and curricula. When the teacher lectures or presents science demonstrations to an entire class, there is relatively little opportunity for the student-to-student interactions that are the strength of the cooperative learning method, or for the independent learning that is the strength of the contract method. At times, however, the demonstration lesson method may be appropriate. These include situations where student laboratory safety is of concern; during review of previous learning; where equipment, supplies, or time is limited; and as prelaboratory instruction for student performance of verification laboratory activities.

Management tasks in the demonstration lesson method

The demonstration lesson method presumes the use of a teacher-centered or modified teacher-centered strategy. Therefore, the management tasks are almost exclusively the responsibility of the teacher, who is responding primarily to extrinsic requirements.

The principal management tasks are as follows:

1. Gather the lesson materials and equipment needed to teach the prescribed themes and topics.
2. Formulate the questions that center on the lecture or teacher demonstration.
3. Provide opportunities for students to restate learned concepts or facts through summary statements and verification laboratories.
4. Bring closure to the topic. Typically, this is done through lesson testing and unit testing, which focuses on students' recall of knowledge and comprehension of learned facts and concepts.

Techniques useful in the demonstration lesson method

Because students are perceived as passive learners, there is a practical limitation on the number of teaching techniques that can be employed in the demonstration lesson. Only the verification laboratory and verification field trip are commonly used.

THE VERIFICATION LABORATORY   A student laboratory, performed after the demonstration lesson, is used to verify the results of the prior teacher demonstration. It is done by one or two students at a learning center or by a whole-class laboratory.

THE VERIFICATION FIELD TRIP   A field trip, taken after the demonstration lesson, is used to review and verify the facts and concepts presented by the teacher. On the field trip, students make observations, write journals, or collect samples that are limited to the topics covered or questions asked by the teacher.

This chapter began with a clarification and discussion of terminology (philosophy, strategy, method, and technique) used to structure effective science teaching. Previous curricula, syllabi, and programs failed to employ consistent terminology and therefore impeded communication between teachers, administrators, and curriculum developers. Such educators might consider the benefits of using the definitions and applications described in this text and summarized in Figure 2-2.

In addition to the theoretical foundation discussed previously, two equally important human aspects of teaching must be considered: flexibility and empathy. Teachers must be flexible enough to select those parts of the philosophies, strategies, methods, and techniques that best match their personality and skills to students' individualized needs. A constructivist-oriented teacher, for example, may have to shift from a pure student-centered strategy to a more teacher-centered strategy if the new strategy would result in increased student mastery of concepts. The same considerations apply to shifts in method and technique used during an instructional period.

The child's social milieu influences his or her ability to benefit from any instructional program. Therefore, teachers must be concerned not only with the child's academic skills but also to external influences on the whole child. Such external influences may affect the teacher's nurturing relationship with each child in terms of mentoring or seeking professional referral actions. Above all, a sense of humor is essential for a satisfying career in teaching.

chapter 3

Problem solving in the elementary science classroom

The essentials: Skills, concepts, and attitudes

Regardless of the instructional philosophy, strategy, method, or technique that is used, one of the most important goals of elementary science education is to prepare students to become effective problem solvers. Activities in this book will enhance students' abilities to achieve that goal. Students who become effective problem solvers will have improved their facility for critical thinking and will be in the process of achieving scientific literacy.

Effective problem solving requires a support structure of grade-appropriate skills (science process, mathematics, and communication skills), conceptual understandings (content mastery), and affective behaviors (values and attitudes). These essentials for successful problem solving are described by Barr (1994). Such problem-solving abilities are nurtured best in student-centered, modified student-centered, and teacher-guided classroom environments. In such classrooms, the techniques of experimentation, library research, field trips, survey research, debates, and model building (Chapter 2, Figure 2-2) each require that students internalize and practice the essentials of problem solving.

The three essential requirements for problem solving can be portrayed as the legs of a stool whose seat represents effective problem-solving ability. This analogy is used in the New York State Elementary Science Syllabus (New York State Education Department, 1984). One leg of the problem-solving support structure is *skills,* defined as the ability to help solve problems by using mathematics, communication arts, science processes, and psychomotor proficiencies. The second leg is *content mastery* through attainment of conceptual understandings. The third leg, *attitudes,* represents the student's value system. In the discussion that follows, the three essential requirements for effective problem solving are referred to as *elements* because, like the elements of nature, they are the building blocks of problem-solving ability.

The skills element

The four skills categories relate to mathematics, communication arts, science process, and psychomotor proficiencies. The ability to measure, graph, estimate, average, and do basic mathematical computations accurately is a prerequisite for learning science. Communication arts are important because they facilitate acquisition of information, either by reading or by listening, and help to communicate one's ideas effectively by writing and speaking. Process skills are the prerequisite for effective experimentation. Students need the cognitive process skills listed in Figure 15-2 (page 157) to help them become effective problem solvers. Psychomotor skills, the final category, are related to students' fine motor abilities such as eye–hand coordination, which enable students to write, use measuring instruments, and manipulate science equipment. Students must be proficient in all four skills categories because they are employed throughout the problem-solving procedure. It is with these tools that students can observe and obtain data from investigations, organize and analyze these data, and generalize from the data to make appropriate decisions.

The conceptual understandings element

Science educators now recognize that the increase in science knowledge exceeds the time available to teach about it. Some science educators fear that if only an activity approach to science is used, we will be sacrificing some of the necessary content. What content topics should be included in a science curriculum that is already too crowded? The three-part answer is simple.

1. Eliminate the minutiae of science, that myriad of meaningless terms that some students memorize and regurgitate on unit tests. Instead, concentrate on the concepts and principles of science. It is more appropriate to teach a little well than to teach a lot poorly.
2. Make the concepts and principles that are included in the curriculum more meaningful and useful to students by having them construct the appropriate concepts primarily by performing science activities. Facts learned without meaning are soon forgotten. How many of us can recall the names of the planets in order from Mercury to Pluto—and how often does this come up in real-life situations? Yet, if we need to know the answer we, as successful problem solvers, would know how to find it.
3. Assess the students' present level of knowledge so that new concepts can be added meaningfully to their repertoire of understandings. Students come to us with experiences in the natural world, and we must build upon these experiences. This is the apperceptive approach to teaching.

The affective behaviors element

Affective behaviors are manifestations of the interrelationship of attitudes and values. Attitudes invariably affect the decisions we make and the types of alternatives we seek. When and where do we develop our attitudes and values? From conversation at the dinner table? From the media? From our colleagues and friends? As educators, we do not wish to impose our values on our students, but we do want to help them develop the ability to examine and interpret situations in order to construct their own system (schema) of values and attitudes.

Using the essentials

As adults, how do we use the elements of problem solving in everyday life? When we go to the supermarket, we walk down aisles packed with a variety of merchandise. Suppose we stop in front of an assortment of dishwashing fluids. Which one do we pick? Do we choose one because we have a coupon for that brand? Do we select the one that the media said was the best? Do we choose one because we like the color, the shape of the bottle, or the cost? At that moment, we make a decision and place the item in our shopping basket. When we use the product, we are testing it. Does its performance meet our expectations? If so, we buy it again. If not, we do not buy it again. In this way, we have used the five-step problem-solving procedure to make an acceptable decision and act on it. This procedure is detailed in the section that follows.

The five-step problem-solving procedure

How can teachers instruct children in the use of the important life skill of problem solving? Based on a review of the problem-solving literature, Kanis (1990) derived a five-step procedure needed for students to identify and arrive at the solution to a problem: (1) defining the problem, (2) devising a plan, (3) implementing the plan, (4) analyzing the data, and (5) making a decision. The problem-solving procedure is diagrammed in Figure 3-1. This procedure encourages individuals to identify bias-free alternatives and to assess the consequences of each alternative in order to decide which one is most socially desirable.

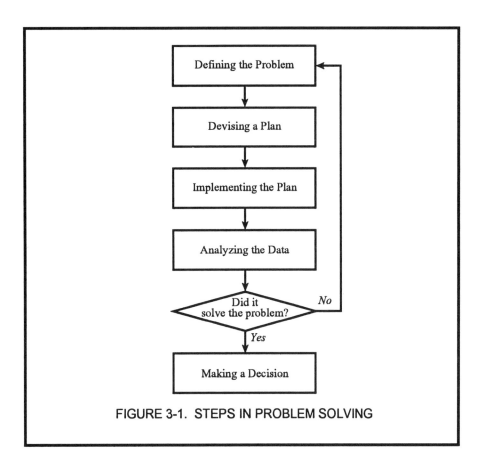

FIGURE 3-1. STEPS IN PROBLEM SOLVING

Science subjects provide an excellent forum in which to educate students in the problem-solving procedure. Our mass media emphasize information about Science, Technology, and Society controversies. Resolving such controversies requires the use of problem-solving strategies. For example, there is a continuing controversy about the fate of the ancient forest of the Pacific Northwest. These trees are a mere fraction of the primeval forest that once reached from coast to coast. Legally, it was not possible to define the problem as preservation of the ancient forest. Instead, the problem was defined as preventing the loss of the spotted owl, an endangered species, which lives in this forest.

The person attempting to solve the problem of preservation of the spotted owl must consider both the national environment and the national economy. If the owl species and its forest habitat were to be preserved, this action might destroy the local logging industry by stopping tree-cutting practices. Alternatively, if the forest were to be clearcut, then the logging industry would flourish for a time, but the owl species might be destroyed. Neither of these alternatives is politically acceptable. Therefore, the next step for the problem solver is to brainstorm acceptable alternatives for resolving the issue. In this case, the alternatives might be selective logging, moving spotted owls to new habitats, or creating new industries to provide jobs for loggers.

After deciding on the alternatives, the problem solver gathers data about each one. Then the problem solver evaluates the consequences of each alternative action and decides which will be of the greatest benefit to both humans and the environment. Finally, the problem solver must act in order to implement the decision.

Teaching the five-step problem-solving procedure

For students to become effective problem solvers, they must do so by solving problems, not merely by watching teachers solve problems. They need exposure to many problems and time to practice solving them. Teachers should recognize that there is no one right way to solve problems. It is hoped, however, that the problem-solving procedure detailed next will serve as a useful guide. By using the five-step problem-solving procedure (Figure 3-1), students will improve their skills, their content mastery, and their ability to clarify attitudes and values.

Presenting the problem

Learning begins with the recognition of a problem. Before a student can solve a problem, he or she must recognize that a problem exists. For ths discussion, a *problem* will be defined as a question or task for which the student cannot immediately see an answer or recall a routine method of finding it.

To teach science as problem solving, teachers must get students involved in the process of doing, hence the need for activities (experiences and/or experimentation). Science activities can be either planned or spontaneous. Planned experiences tend to be used where teacher-centered strategies are being employed. In contrast, spontaneous experiences are those that may arise from student discussions or may be the unplanned result of problems that arise during a planned exercise in more student-centered classrooms. The experiences, whether planned or spontaneous, should stimulate curiosity and create a need to know.

Planned experiences may help with initial efforts to orient students in the problem-solving procedure. There are two basic ways of introducing a planned problem:

1. Presenting problem-solving introductory statements or questions
2. Presenting a discrepant event

Both of these types of problem introductions, commonly called *motivators* in lesson planning, are discussed next.

Introductory statements

Gott and Murphy (1987) have suggested a variety of introductory statements for problem solving. In contrast, the "explain why" type of question may not be an appropriate motivator because it is often used as an assessment question that relies on prior acquisition of concepts, or as an aim in many teacher-centered classrooms. Gott's introductory statements include the following.

Decide which . . .

This type of problem asks students to make a choice—for example, "Decide which chocolate chip cookie is the best."

Find a way to . . .

This type of problem envisions a situation in which no obvious solution exists—for example, "Find a way to weigh an elephant on a bathroom scale."

Find the effect of . . .

This type of problem may involve the manipulation of one or more variables and the discovery of the interaction of one on the other—for example, "What is the effect of the height of water in a can on the rate at which the water emerges from a hole in the side of the can?"

Find the cause of . . .

This type of problem may deal with cause-and-effect relationships—for example, "Find the cause of the failure of a bulb to light in a simple series electric circuit."

Make a structure, or machine . . .

An example of this type of problem is, "Use drinking straws and paper clips to make a structure that will support a brick."

Discrepant events

A more sophisticated, problem-initiating activity is the presentation of a discrepant event. *Discrepant events* are experiences that demonstrate unexpected or unusual results. They pose conflicts, differences, disagreements, disharmonies, and inconsistencies for the observer. Teachers must use experiences already in the students' repertoire to help them recognize that a discrepant event is a problem. These discrepancies, in turn, get students to ask questions that will help them to define the problem. For example, blowing across a horizontal strip of paper with one end held up against one's chin will cause the far end to rise. The average student would expect the air flow to push the end of the paper downward. The opposite behavior of the paper is the discrepant event.

In Piagetian terms, we are causing a disequilibrium with prior student experiences. During disequilibrium, the student begins to sense contradictions in his or her reasoning processes. This breakdown in a child's intellectual schema is usually followed by a reorganization of thought patterns. Accordingly, in these disequilibria are important factors in the acquisition of knowledge and lifelong learning.

Piagetian scholars also believe that a child actively constructs knowledge internally through continual interaction with the environment, rather than by passively absorbing knowledge. The constructivist philosophy, discussed in Chapter 2, is interpreted by science educators to mean that we must facilitate as many concrete experiences as possible for students. It is obvious that emphasizing experiences with hands-on materials that can be examined and manipulated will aid in concept formation. Only from this point may we begin to depart from the concrete experience and to use symbolic materials and experiences to facilitate formal operational reasoning.

Presenting the five-step procedure

Each step in the problem-solving procedure, shown in Figure 3-1 and described next, requires students to employ the three elements (skills, conceptual understandings, and affective behaviors) required for effective problem solving. If students are weak in one of the elements, then using the five-step procedure should strengthen the area of deficiency.

Step 1. Defining the problem

In constructivist-oriented classrooms, the problem-solving questions will arise from student interests. In expertist-oriented classrooms, teachers may wish to use the problem-solving introductory statement discussed previously. In either case, it is crucial that students be able to state the problem in their own words. Students should then discuss and brainstorm precise questions arising from the problem statement.

A decision must be made as to whether all student groups will attempt to answer one question or whether different groups will attempt to answer different questions. The decision is based on the pedagogical method emphasized by the teacher.

Step 2. Devising a plan

Students are now at the second step of the problem-solving procedure. In devising a plan, the first action is to answer the following six questions, which have been modified from the New York State Education Department's *Elementary Science Syllabus* (1984):

1. What background information do I already have?
2. What new information do I need, and how will I acquire it?
3. Which technique (experimentation, library or survey research, debate, etc.) must I use?
4. What sequence of steps must I follow when using the chosen technique?
5. Which materials or human resources will I need to complete the task and/or answer the question?
6. How will I know when I have solved the problem?

In this stage, students should anticipate the advantages and disadvantages of each solution or plan as well as making predictions about the possible results of completing the plan.

Step 3. Implementing the plan

The next step is carrying out the plan. Here students need to gather their materials and implement the plan by using one or more of the techniques (experimentation, library or survey research, debate, etc.) described in Chapter 2. In this step, students begin to explore and/or construct conceptual understandings.

Step 4. Analyzing the data

During the fourth step in problem solving, the student will organize and analyze the data. Here, organization of data can, at best, be addressed only tentatively because the original plan for organization of the accumulated data may not be useful. The format (tables, charts, and graphs) can be deemed useful only when the problem solver begins to analyze the data. When analyzing the data, the student needs to find patterns in the data. Does the perceived pattern help to solve the problem, or does it raise other possibilities? At this point, the problem solver may need to change the plan or use a different form of organizing the data. The diamond-shaped block in Figure 3-1 presents the question, "Did the first four steps of the procedure lead to a solution of the problem?" If the technique leads to an apparent solution and there are no further questions, the student proceeds to the decision-making step. If, however, the problem is not solved, then there is a need for feedback to clarify the problem or question. After such clarification, the problem-solving procedure is repeated.

Step 5. Making a decision

Decision making is the final step in the problem-solving procedure. To make such a final decision, the problem solver should address the following four affective-domain questions, which are based on the New York State Education Department's Elementary Science Syllabus (1984):

1. Which values relate to each possible decision, and what is the relationship?
2. Which are the alternative choices, and what are the consequences of each alternative?
3. Who will be affected by each possible choice and in what way?
4. Which choice is the best choice?

The final decision may lead directly to a plan of action, or it may reveal other problems to be solved by the five-step procedure.

Using the problem-solving procedure with student activities

The problem-solving procedure discussed here is fundamental regardless of the technique (experimentation, library or survey research, debate, etc.) being used. Because this is an activity-oriented book, however, the five-step problem-solving procedure is used indirectly. A comparison of steps in the problem-solving procedure and their equivalent steps using student investigations is shown in Figure 3-2.

FIVE-STEP PROBLEM-SOLVING PROCEDURE	EQUIVALENT STEPS USING STUDENT INVESTIGATIONS
1. Defining the Problem	Problem Statement
2. Devising the Plan	Materials
3. Implementing the Plan	Getting Started
4. Analyzing the Data	Suggested Critical Thinking Questions
5. Making a Decision	Statement of Constructed Concept or Plan of Action

FIGURE 3-2.   COMPARISON OF FIVE-STEP PROBLEM-SOLVING PROCEDURE AND EQUIVALENT STEPS USING STUDENT INVESTIGATIONS

Activities presented in this book begin with a problem statement. This is the first step in the problem-solving procedure as diagrammed in Figure 3-1. The second and third steps, "devising the plan" and "implementing the plan," are fulfilled by the listing of materials and the information contained in the "Getting Started" section of the activity. The "Suggested Critical Thinking Questions" help with the fourth step of the problem-solving procedure, "analyzing the data." That is, the "Suggested Critical Thinking Questions" may be discussed with students at this time to aid in concept development. These question responses should elicit the information found in the "Background" section of the investigation. After analyzing the data, the student reaches step 5 (making a decision) in which he or she states the science concept constructed from analysis of results of the investigation. The student-constructed concept should be the answer to the problem statement that was framed, in the form of a question, as the title of the activity. However, evidence of student mastery of learned concepts is demonstrated only by the students' ability to apply the concepts to new situations.

Example #1

In Chapter 5, the K–2 students perform an investigation titled "What causes us to have day and night?" The constructed concept resulting from this investigation is that the earth's rotation on its axis causes day and night. For the children, acquisition of this concept should help to dispel the ancient misconception that the sun revolves around the earth.

To assess mastery of the earth rotation–day/night concept, the students might be asked to observe the location of the sun at sunrise and sunset. Then they would be asked to explain or demonstrate how the concept of the earth's rotation explains what appears to be the movement of the sun through the sky.

If, however, the student investigation had implications for Science, Technology, and Society issues, then the constructed concepts still would answer the problem statement that is the title of the activity. More immediately, however, analysis of the data could be used to formulate a plan of action that would address the four affective questions, listed previously, that lead to decision making.

Example #2

The spotted owl controversy discussed earlier could lead to many problem-solving activities and constructed concepts. Suppose that one of the constructed concepts that arose from this Science, Technology, and Society–related investigation led to the conclusion that continued logging in this mountainous area of ancient forest would result in unacceptable rates of erosion and downslope sedimentation. A concern might be that the sediment could contaminate a larger river that supplies drinking water, or that it could smother fish breeding grounds or clog a reservoir downstream. Therefore, the Science, Technology, and Society nature of the investigation requires that a plan of action be devised to prevent such erosion and sediment movement in areas where logging will continue. The plan of action might require that replanting of the forest should immediately follow logging operations. Or the plan of action might call for sediment catch basins to be constructed so that the sediment would not have an adverse impact on the surroundings.

Because most Science, Technology, and Society issues are multifaceted, many concepts will arise even from relatively simple issues. Each concept will lead to a plan of action and continued investigations. Therefore, an entire class can be actively engaged in investigating and planning solutions to Science, Technology, and Society issues.

chapter 4

How to use this book

Activity format

This K–6 earth science activity book is designed as a supplement to standard elementary science texts. It can also be used as a stand-alone teaching guide and activity resource. It provides the practitioner with activities that have been newly created or revised from proven classroom investigations. Each chapter presents the concepts needed to understand an important theme of earth science. The activities are presented in a manner that is appropriate to the cognitive level and motor skills of students in the designated grades. The materials recommended are readily available and can be easily manipulated by students. The activities and their related "Suggested Critical Thinking Questions" encourage the students to construct or expand on appropriate concepts. In addition, these activities may help students to become aware of Science, Technology, and Society problems and to participate in the search for viable solutions to them.

A teacher might want to use an activity at the beginning of a lesson as a motivator. Another teacher might use the activity as the core of the lesson and then elicit appropriate science concepts either from discussion of the activity or by formal questioning techniques. Teachers in student-centered classrooms might use the activities in this book to seek solutions to student-identified problems.

In the book, each earth science concept is presented at three grade groupings: K–2, 3–4, and 5–6. Each grade grouping carries an activity title that can serve as a problem statement. The activity then leads students to the solution of the problem. A teacher background section contains the grade-appropriate science concepts and terminology, which helps the teacher to understand the problem. In a teacher-centered classroom, this background information can be given to the students. In a more student-centered classroom, such background information can be elicited from students either during or after their involvement in the activity. A glossary (in the Teacher Support Section) gives functional definitions of new words that are underlined in the background text.

This book presents the recurring conceptual themes of earth science in a sequence that allows for use of the outdoors for extensions of some investigations when the weather is appropriate. One or more diagrams are included to show the physical arrangement of the materials used in the investigation. The next section of text, "Getting Started," is provided to the teacher to facilitate setup and performance of the investigation.

The last section of each investigation contains "Suggested Critical Thinking Questions." These questions are sequential in that they lead students to concept formation and an internalization that provides solution of the initial problem. Also, the questions involve the students in higher level thinking processes. Teachers should consider these "Suggested Critical Thinking Questions" to be a model of appropriate questioning technique. The K–2 student group may have difficulty with some of the science process skills terms (like *predict*) in the "Suggested Critical Thinking Questions." Using the term *educated guess* as a synonym for *prediction* allows students to define the term operationally. In this case, the term *educated guess* refers to applying prior experience and knowledge to imagine the results of an activity (experiment). In such questions, the word *predict* or *prediction* is followed by (*guess*) as shorthand for *educated guess*. Employing operational definitions for many of the terms used in thinking about science will allow elementary students to internalize the meanings of such words and further enhance their ability to construct concepts.

The "Suggested Critical Thinking Questions" can be used in a dialogue with student groups during the investigation or in a summary discussion. However, teachers may want to generate their own questions, even including lower level knowledge and comprehension questions as appropriate to student needs.

Using the cooperative learning method

Cooperative learning, one of the teaching methods discussed in Chapter 2, is singled out here for further discussion because it provides empowerment for students. It not only should increase students' science concept development and process skills but also should enable them to integrate such learning with other subjects and to refine their socialization skills.

Activities in this book have been written to allow flexibility in use as teacher demonstrations, individual investigations, or small-group investigations where the cooperative learning method can achieve its highest potential. However, the activities specify the number of students per group on the basis of only two considerations: (1) the number of experimental setups needed per class and (2) the efficiency of classroom management. The students in the specified group for each activity can have one or more of the five cooperative learning roles listed in Chapter 2: materials handler, experimenter, recorder, reporter, and researcher (to gather information from ancillary sources). For some of the activities in this book, the role of researcher may not need to be filled.

The following is an example of how to adapt the activities in this book to facilitate cooperative learning. The grade 3–4 wind vane activity (Chapter 7) needs to involve a minimum of two students. Jointly, they construct a device that indicates the direction from which the wind blows. Then they practice using it. To use the cooperative learning method with this activity, the two students will adopt more than one role. For example, the materials handler also can be the recorder, and the experimenter also can be the reporter. Both students may do research on the design and use of wind direction indicators for long-term and short-term weather studies. When each of the class groups has completed the wind vane activity, selected reporters (or all of them) will contribute to a classroom discussion of all aspects of the activity. The teacher acts as facilitator of the discussion, contributes by dispelling any misconceptions about the science concepts needed to understand the activity, and helps to bring closure to this instructional segment.

Suppose, however, that the class goal is to observe and record all aspects of weather by building a weather station. Then each group could build one weather instrument, demonstrate and discuss its use with the entire class, and contribute to fabrication of the weather station. In this case, the effort of each small cooperative group contributes to the goal of the larger cooperative group. Construction of two other instruments for the weather station is done through the grade 3–4 activities in Chapter 7. The teacher management tasks throughout each step in the weather station project remain as described here.

Assessing readiness for activities and mastery of concepts

The activities in the book use spiral approach to concept acquisition. That is, basic concepts, investigated at a lower grade level for each theme, are followed by investigations of more advanced related concepts at higher grade levels. Early childhood teachers may wish to assess student readiness for conducting activities by brainstorming. During the brainstorming session, the teachers elicit information about relevant ideas or concepts from students. Such information reveals students' conceptions or misconceptions and allows for peer teaching. The teacher can then pursue avenues of student-suggested inquiry. This may lead to using an appropriate activity from this book.

Upper elementary school teachers may choose to use the earlier investigation(s) with their students as a means of assessing prior knowledge. Evidence of mastery of the basic concepts would suggest that the students are capable of negotiating their grade-appropriate investigations. If students demonstrate a deficiency in conceptual understandings related to the earth science theme under discussion, the teacher must begin the unit of study with review or reinforcement protocol.

Each activity and its accompanying "Suggested Critical Thinking Questions" may be used if your current textbook does not include investigations appropriate for a particular concept. If you have used other investigations to explore the same earth science concepts, then you can use targeted investigations from this book as part of an authentic testing protocol. More information on authentic testing is found in Chapter 15.

part two

Earth Science Activities Based on Major Themes

chapter 5

There are predictable relationships between the sun, earth, and moon

| *What causes us to have day and night?*

Background

The *earth* is the third *planet* from the *sun* in our *solar system*. Life exists on earth because of our location in the solar system and our *atmosphere*. Life forms have not been found on any other planet.

The sun's visible light gives us daylight. Darkness occurs when there is no daylight. When daylight is present, we call it *day*. When darkness is present, we call it *night*.

Day and night occur at each place on the earth because the earth turns toward, or away from, the sun in an easterly direction. The earth has an imaginary north–south *axis* on which it turns; this motion is called *rotation*. The north end of this imaginary north–south line is called the *north geographic pole*. The south end is called the *south geographic pole*. When you are in a place on the earth that is facing the sun, you have day. When you are in a place that is facing away from the sun, then you have night.

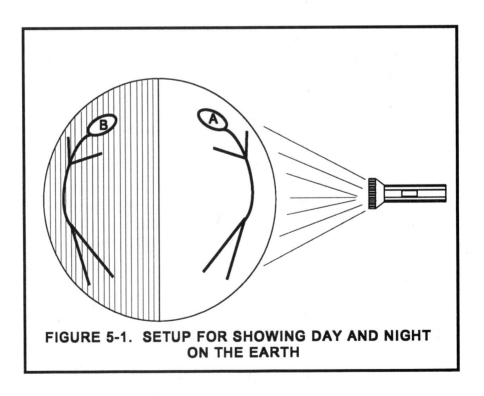

FIGURE 5-1. SETUP FOR SHOWING DAY AND NIGHT ON THE EARTH

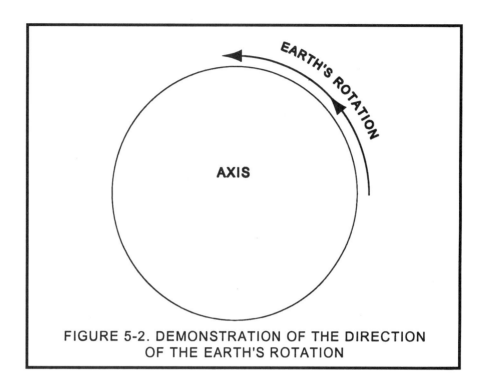

FIGURE 5-2. DEMONSTRATION OF THE DIRECTION
OF THE EARTH'S ROTATION

Figure 5-1 illustrates the setup for showing day and night on the earth. Figure 5-2 shows a demonstration of the direction of the earth's rotation.

Materials

Per group of 4–6 students:

    12" ball
    two 4" cardboard stick figures
    flashlight
    cellophane tape
    marking pen

Getting started

Part 1

   1. Students tape two 4" tall stick figures to opposite sides of the 12" ball.

2. Students use the marking pen to label one stick figure Person A and one Person B.
3. Darken the room so that the flashlight illuminates Person A on the ball.

Suggested critical thinking questions

Part 1

1. Where does the light in the sky come from?
2. If it is daytime for Person A, what part of the day is it for Person B? What makes you think that?
3. How do we get Person B into the daylight without moving the flashlight?
4. Why wasn't moving the flashlight an acceptable answer?
5. Where is the sun at night?
6. How does the earth move so that a person goes through a day followed by a night?

Getting started

Part 2

1. Students place the 12" ball on a flat surface so that they can look down on the top of the ball.
2. Students spin the ball in place so that the ball spins in a counterclockwise direction (in the correct direction of the earth's rotation).

Suggested critical thinking questions

Part 2

1. If you lay your bicycle on the ground and spin the wheel, what do you call the part of the wheel around which it spins?
2. Can you find a place on the top of the ball that looks like everything is spinning (rotating) around it? What place on the earth does this represent?
3. If the ball is turned upside down and rotated again, is there another place on the ball that looks like everything is rotating around it? What place on the earth does this represent?

The moon: Why do we see it sometimes and not at other times?

Background

The *moon* is a *natural satellite* of the *earth*. The moon rotates on its axis only once each *month* (29.5 days) while revolving around the earth once in the same time period. As a result, we can see only a little more than half of the moon. The far side of the moon can never be seen from earth. However, moon-orbiting *satellites* have taken pictures of the far side of the moon.

Only about half of the earth sphere is illuminated by the sun at any time. The same is true of our moon or any other planet in the solar system. Because of the moon's position in its orbit around the earth, the amount of the illuminated half that we can observe changes from a fully illuminated half to a nonilluminated (dark) half moon. Even though it is dark, it is the same side of the moon that is facing the earth. In between are the *waning* and *waxing phases* of the moon, as shown in Figure 5-3.

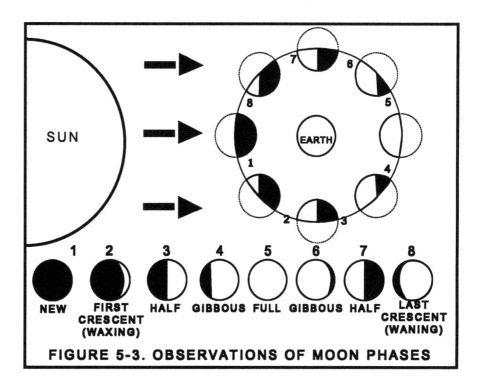

FIGURE 5-3. OBSERVATIONS OF MOON PHASES

Materials

Per group of 4 students:

large ball or globe to represent the earth
smaller ball to represent the moon
flashlight to represent the sun
worksheet to draw 8 phases of the moon (same as shown in
   the lower half of Figure 5-3, but all circles are blank and
   are not labeled)
3-foot length of string with chalk attached

Getting started

1. The teacher uses the chalk and string to draw a 6-foot diameter circle for each group.
2. The teacher divides the circumference of each circle into eight 2-foot lengths and then numbers the end of each segment from #1 through #8 in a counterclockwise direction (Figure 5-3).
3. One student, representing the earth, holds the ball (globe) on his or her head and stands in the center of the circle.
4. A second student, representing the moon, stands on the numbers drawn on the circumference, beginning with #1. This student will always face the center of the circle.
5. A third student holds the flashlight and stands in one spot 3 feet away from the drawn circumference of the circle.
6. A fourth student stands next to the person at the center. Using the worksheet, this person draws the shape of the illuminated part of the moon that he or she and the earth person see.
7. The earth person turns in a counterclockwise direction to face each number on the circumference line in sequence, beginning with #1.
8. The moon person moves to the number position that the earth person is facing.
9. The third person remains on the original spot and shines the flashlight on the moon.
10. The recorder draws the shape of the illuminated part of the moon in the numbered box on the worksheet.
11. The earth person turns to the next higher number, and the moon person moves to face him or her. The recorder again draws the illuminated section of the moon on the worksheet.

Suggested critical thinking questions

1. How would you position the sun, earth, and moon to demonstrate that different amounts of the moon's face are illuminated during the month?
2. If the earth person rotated once while doing the activity, how many times would the moon person rotate?
3. How can you prove from this activity that the same side of the moon always faces the earth?
4. What causes the moon to shine?
5. Why did American astronauts land only on the sunny side of the moon?

Why do the moon and the earth cast shadows on each other?

Background

The moon revolves around the earth every 29.5 days. Sometimes the moon is in a position between the earth and the sun so that it briefly blocks the sun's light for some people on earth. During such times people are in the moon's shadow. This is called a *solar eclipse*.

In contrast, sometimes the earth is between the sun and the moon so that the earth's shadow falls on the moon. This is called a *lunar eclipse*. Eclipses are relatively rare because they require the earth, sun, and moon to be lined up on the same plane.

During a solar eclipse, a small portion of the earth is completely in the dark of the moon's shadow *(umbra)*. Because of the angle of the sun's rays, however, nearby areas experience only a partial eclipse *(penumbra)*. The umbra and penumbra shadows result from the crossing of the sunlight rays, which travel in straight lines in all directions from all parts of the sun's surface.

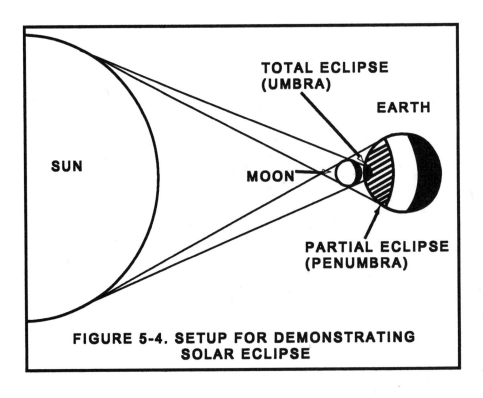

FIGURE 5-4. SETUP FOR DEMONSTRATING SOLAR ECLIPSE

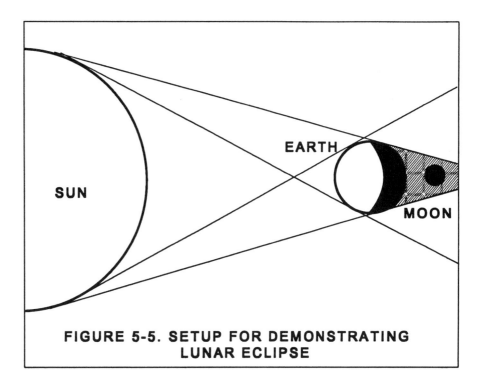

FIGURE 5-5. SETUP FOR DEMONSTRATING LUNAR ECLIPSE

Figure 5-4 illustrates a setup for demonstrating a solar eclipse, and Figure 5-5 shows a setup for demonstrating a lunar eclipse.

Materials

Per group of 3 students:

>   globe or 12″ ball
>   tennis ball
>   flashlight

Getting started

1. The teacher darkens the room.
2. The student representing the sun shines the flashlight on the simulated moon, which is positioned 2 feet in front of the earth ball (globe). The second student holds both balls. The third student records the observations.
3. The student representing the sun shines the flashlight on the simulated earth, which is positioned 2 feet in front of the moon. The third student records the observations.

Suggested critical thinking questions

1. How can you position the sun and the moon so that the moon casts a shadow on the earth to simulate a solar eclipse?
2. How can you position the sun and the earth so that the earth casts a shadow on the moon to simulate a lunar eclipse?
3. During which phases of the moon is it possible to have a solar eclipse?
4. Why do some people experience a total solar eclipse at the same time that others are experiencing a partial solar eclipse?

chapter 6

The daily and yearly earth-sun relationships cause changes in air temperature

How are daily temperature changes caused by changes in sunlight?

Background

Sunlight causes heating of the earth's surface. Then the warm earth heats the air near the surface. Therefore, the earth and the air become warmer during the day and cool off at night.

The relative strength of sunlight (see the activity for grades 3–4) and length of the day are greatest in the summer season. Therefore, the earth's surface becomes very warm in summer, and the air above it reaches a maximum temperature. Such conditions are reversed during the winter season.

Figure 6-1 shows a setup for investigating changes in air temperature.

Materials

Per group of 4 students:

> 2 plastic-backed alcohol thermometers
> two 1-pint milk or plastic containers, one filled with cold water, one filled with warm tap water
> 1 set of pictures showing people on a beach and people playing in the snow
> 1 clear 2-liter plastic soda bottle with its top 5" cut off
> 1 tray at least 5" square, filled with at least 1" of dry potting soil
> masking tape
> marking pen
> 100-watt light bulb and reflector housing

Getting started

Part 1

1. The teacher uses masking tape to cover any temperature graduations on each thermometer. The thermometer bulb and glass tube should remain exposed.

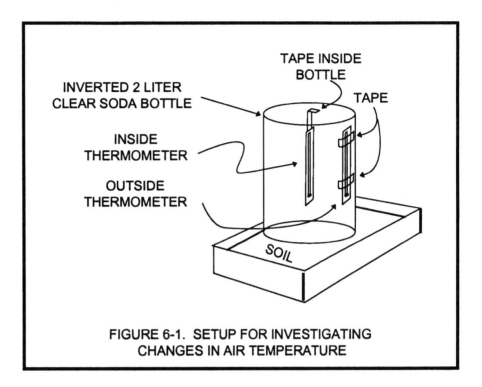

FIGURE 6-1. SETUP FOR INVESTIGATING
CHANGES IN AIR TEMPERATURE

2. Students place the thermometer into a container of cold water for 30 seconds and mark the level of (red) alcohol on masking tape.
3. Students repeat this procedure with warm water.
4. The teacher uses a large demonstration thermometer to generalize about the relationship between "warm/cold" and temperature as represented by the level of red liquid in the glass tube.
5. The teacher assesses student mastery of the heat–temperature relationship by having students draw thermometers that show relative temperatures that might be recorded at the beach during the summer and in snowy environments during the winter.

Suggested critical thinking questions

Part 1

1. How does the position of the red liquid in the thermometer change when the thermometer bulb is held between your palms? Why does this happen?
2. What is a thermometer? Where is it used? What does it tell us?
3. Predict (guess) what will happen to the position of the red liquid in the thermometer when the thermometer bulb is placed in the cold water. Was your prediction (guess) correct? Why or why not?

4. Predict (guess) what will happen to the position of the red liquid in the thermometer when the thermometer bulb is placed in warm water. Was your prediction (guess) correct? Why or why not?

5. What is the relationship between heat and cold and the position of the red liquid in the thermometer?

Getting started

Part 2

1. The teacher prepares a soil-filled tray for each student group and places the trays under individual 100-watt bulbs for at least half an hour before the lesson. Bulbs should be protected in a reflector housing unit with a cage or other provision to prevent burns.

2. The teacher cuts 5″ off the top of each 1-liter soda bottle (tops can be saved for later use as funnels).

3. The teacher tapes one thermometer on the inside top of the soda bottle, suspended from the center. The bulb should point toward the open end of the soda bottle (1½″ from the cut end).

4. A second thermometer is similarly taped on the outside of the soda bottle (1½″ from the cut end) close to the inside thermometer and facing in the same direction.

5. Students use markers to indicate the level of red liquid on both thermometers (the liquid level for the inside thermometer is marked on the surface of the bottle). This is done before the soda bottle is placed over the soil.

6. The tray of soil is removed from sunlight. Students place the open end of the soda bottle on top of the soil and wait at least one minute before marking new liquid levels for the thermometers.

7. Leave the tray of soil and bottle in position and wait at least 15 minutes before recording (marking) the thermometer liquid levels again.

Suggested critical thinking questions

Part 2

1. What do you think will happen to the temperature of the soil exposed to the heat from the light bulb? Is your guess confirmed by touching the soil?

2. Predict what will happen to the liquid levels in the thermometers after the soda bottle is placed on the soil. Was your prediction correct? Why or why not?

3. What is the relation between the temperature of air in the soda bottle and the temperature of the soil?

4. Predict what will happen to the air temperature in the soda bottle as time goes by. Was your prediction correct? Why or why not?

5. How does your answer to question 4 help explain why you might need a sweater or a blanket at night?

Why is the sun's warmth greater in the summer than in the winter?

Background

In the United States, the sun is higher in the sky during the summer than in the winter. Therefore, its rays are more concentrated at the earth's surface. Such intense sunlight causes extreme warming of soil and rock. Also, there are more hours of available sunlight in the summer season to warm soil and rocks (see the activity for grades 5–6). In contrast, during the winter the sun is lower in the sky. Therefore, its rays are less concentrated and there are fewer hours of sunlight. As a result, there is little warming of soil and rock.

Figure 6-2 shows a setup for determining seasonal solar heating effects, and Figure 6-3 is a data sheet for recording solar heating effects.

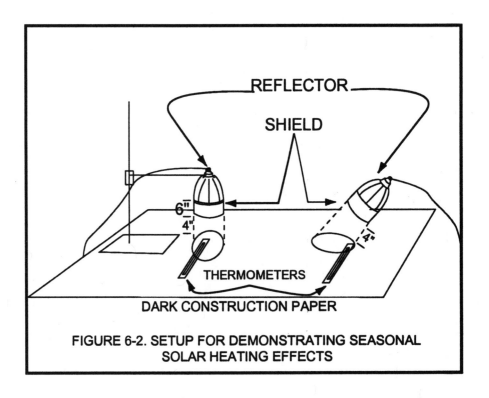

FIGURE 6-2. SETUP FOR DEMONSTRATING SEASONAL SOLAR HEATING EFFECTS

LAMP VERTICAL		LAMP AT 45° ANGLE	
Initial temperature		Initial temperature	
2-minute temperature		2-minute temperature	
3-minute temperature		3-minute temperature	
4-minute temperature		4-minute temperature	

FIGURE 6-3   DATA SHEET FOR RECORDING SOLAR HEATING EFFECTS

Materials

Per group of 4–6 students:

two 5″–6″-diameter screw-on aluminum reflectors

Safety hint: Warn students not to touch the reflectors because they can cause skin burns when in use.

2 bulb base/clamp assemblies
2 100-watt incandescent bulbs
3 thermometers
2 oak tag strips (6″ wide x 18″ long)
masking tape
four 8½″ x 11″ pieces of dark-colored construction paper (to cover the desk)
2 ring stands or chairs whose backs are at least 12″ above the tabletop
chalk
watch with a second hand
12″ ruler
data sheet (Figure 6-3)

Getting started

Part 1

1. The teacher should prepare 6" x 18" oak tag strips and tape them around each reflector as a shield to help direct the beams of light.
2. Students should set up materials as shown in the diagram and prepare (or receive) a data sheet.
3. The bottom of the shield should be 4" from the construction paper for both vertical and 45-degree lamp orientation (see Figure 6-2).
4. Turn on the light of the vertical lamp, record the thermometer temperature, and place the thermometer bulb in the center of the illuminated area. Take and record 1-minute temperature readings for a total of 4 minutes.
5. Use chalk to outline the illuminated area.

Part 2

1. Turn on the lamp that is angled at 45 degrees to the table top. Record the temperature and place the thermometer bulb inside the edge of the illuminated area (4" from the bottom of the shield). Take and record 1-minute temperature readings for a total of 4 minutes.
2. Use chalk to outline the illuminated area.

Suggested critical thinking questions

1. Predict the relationship between the duration (length of time) the vertical light is shining and the temperature of the thermometer. Does your result support your prediction? Why or why not?
2. Do you think the results from the angled (45-degree) lamp will be the same or different from the results with the vertical lamp? Explain.
3. Do the results from the angled lamp support your prediction? Why or why not?
4. How do the outlines of the illuminated areas compare? How do these differences help to explain the temperature results from the two lamps?

5. Explain the relationship between the length of time both lamps were on and the four 1-minute temperature readings.

6. Given that days are longer in the summer and that the sun is higher in the sky, how do your results help to explain the difference in the earth's surface temperature from summer to winter?

Why is it winter in the United States when it is summer in Australia?

Background

As the earth orbits the sun, its *axis* remains pointed toward the star *Polaris*. Therefore, the sun's rays are directed more toward the *Northern Hemisphere* in our summer (the sun's rays are more intense), and our hours of daylight are increased. These two factors result in warm summer temperatures (see the activity for grades 3–4). In contrast, the sun's rays are directed more toward the *Southern Hemisphere* in our winter (the sun's rays are less intense), and the hours of daylight are decreased. These two factors result in cool winter temperatures.

Because the earth's *orbit* around the sun is an *ellipse,* we are slightly closer to the sun in our winter than in our summer. However, the increased amount of heat from the sun that results from its relative closeness to the earth is offset by the sun's rays being directed more toward the Southern Hemisphere. The result is slanting sun rays, which have a lessened heating effect on the Northern Hemisphere.

Figure 6-4 shows a setup for simulating solar heating during winter in the Northern Hemisphere.

Materials

Per group of 4–6 students:

    12" globe or ball
    3 alcohol-filled thermometers or fever thermometers
    5"–6" diameter lamp with reflector
    bulb base/clip-on device
    100-watt bulb
    12" ruler
    cellophane tape
    ring stand or chair whose back is about 12" above table top

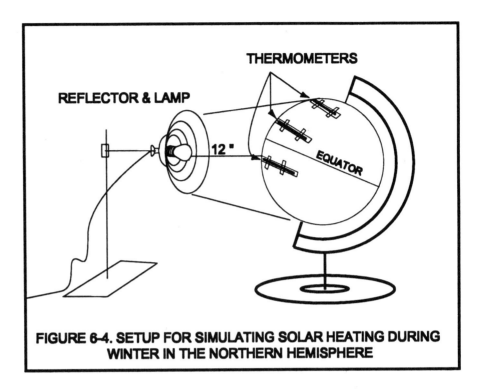

FIGURE 6-4. SETUP FOR SIMULATING SOLAR HEATING DURING WINTER IN THE NORTHERN HEMISPHERE

Getting started

1. Students set up the bulb base/clip-on device and reflector so that the reflector is in line with the middle of the globe and 12" away from its surface.
2. Students tape one thermometer onto the globe directly in line with the reflector (middle of globe). Students tape a second thermometer at the highest point on the globe, directly above the first. They tape the third thermometer equidistant between the other two and in line with them (see Figure 6-4).
3. For each thermometer, students make a table on which they can record the initial temperature and temperature for four 1-minute intervals (after the light is turned on).

Suggested critical thinking questions

1. Predict the relationship between temperature and location of the thermometers on the surface of the globe. Do your data support your prediction? Why or why not?
2. What is the relationship between the earth's position in its orbit and the intensity of sunlight at the earth's surface?

3. What is the relationship between the earth's position in its orbit and the length of the day?

4. How does the combination of sunlight intensity and length of day determine which hemisphere is having summer and which is having winter? Explain.

5. If the earth is closer to the sun in our winter, what effect does that have on our winter temperatures?

chapter 7

Weather results from changes in air movement, temperature, and humidity

| *What type of day is best for drying clothes outdoors?*

Background

Air is all around us. Its temperature will change if it is heated or cooled. Air can take up and give back some water from its surroundings (*evaporation* and *condensation*). The warmer the air, the faster it will take up moisture. When moist air comes in contact with cold surfaces, it will give up some of its moisture to form a haze or water droplets on the cold surfaces. The amount of water that the air can hold is called its *humidity*. Air moving across the earth's surface is called *wind*. Wind causes faster evaporation because it carries more air past wet surfaces.

Figure 7-1 shows a setup for studying evaporation and condensation.

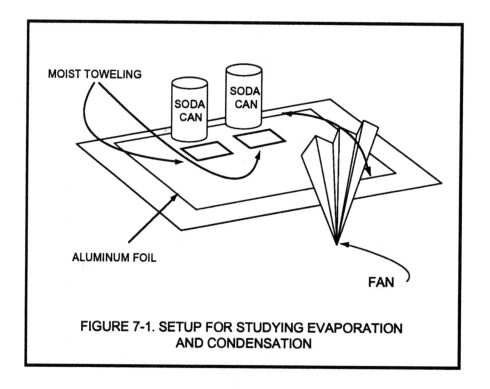

FIGURE 7-1. SETUP FOR STUDYING EVAPORATION AND CONDENSATION

Materials

Per group of 2 students:

8½″ x 11″ construction paper for the fan
6″ x 6″ piece of aluminum foil
two 2″ x 2″ pieces of paper toweling
eye dropper
2 cans of soda (1 cold, 1 at room temperature)
cellophane tape

Getting started

1. The teacher tapes aluminum foil to each desk and then tapes the two pieces of paper toweling to the center of the aluminum foil (taping only left and right sides of the paper toweling allows the breeze from the fan to go over and under the paper toweling).
2. Students make the fan.
3. Students place the soda cans close to the far edge of the pieces of paper toweling.
4. Students put one drop of water at the center of each piece of paper toweling.
5. One student fans across the paper toweling, toward the cans, for 1 minute while the other student observes the fronts of the cans.

Suggested critical thinking questions

1. What is your prediction (guess) about what will happen to the damp pieces of paper toweling when you fan across them? Was your prediction (guess) correct? Why or why not?
2. What is your prediction (guess) about how the outside of the cans will change as you fan over the damp pieces of paper toweling? Was your prediction (guess) correct? Why or why not?
3. What is your prediction (guess) about the relationship between the temperature of the two cans and the changes that you observed on the outside of each can?
4. Where did the water go when you fanned across the damp paper toweling? Did any water pass through the aluminum foil? How do you know?
5. Why does wet wash become dry when it is put out on the clothesline? Would it dry faster on a warm day or a cooler day? Why do you think so? Would it dry faster on a windy day or a calm day? Why do you think so?

How are wind direction, wind speed, and rainfall measured?

Background

Wind is the horizontal flow of air from a *high-pressure area* to a *low-pressure area*. High-pressure areas form where the air is cooled. Cool air weighs more than warm air, so it sinks and spreads out over the earth's surface. Low-pressure areas form where air is warmed. Warm air weighs less than cool air, so it rises. (An instrument for measuring air pressure, a *barometer*, is constructed as one of the grade 5–6 activities).

Wind direction is indicated by a *wind vane*, whose point (head) shows the direction from which the wind is blowing. This wind direction is named by the compass direction from which it flows; e.g., a northwest wind comes from the northwest direction.

Wind speed is measured by an *anemometer*. Commonly used anemometers have three horizontal cups that rotate on a vertical shaft. The rate of rotation gives a measure of wind speed.

Atmospheric moisture will *condense* into raindrops when the air is cooled. The height (depth) of the water accumulation resulting from each fainfall is measured by an instrument called a *rain gauge*. A cuplike container in the rain gauge is *calibrated* so that the height of water in the cup equals the amount of rainfall.

Figure 7-2 shows how to assemble a wind vane.

Materials

For use with the whole class:

  electric fan

Part 1: Wind vane

Per group of 2 students:

¼" x 12" wood dowel stick
push pin

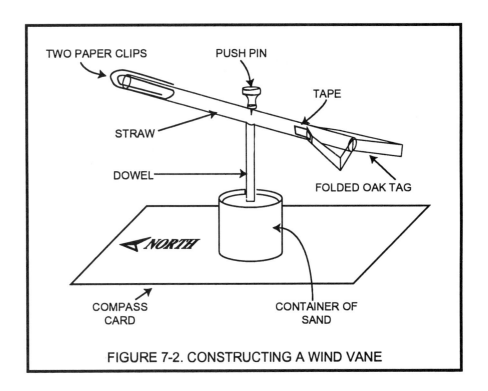

FIGURE 7-2. CONSTRUCTING A WIND VANE

8" straw
2" x 6" oak tag strip
2 paper clips
plastic jar filled with sand or soil
5" x 8" index card with compass directions indicated
cellophane tape

Getting started

Part 1: Wind vane

1. Students assemble the wind vane as shown in Figure 7-2.
2. The card with compass directions is geographically oriented on students' desks, and the wind vane is placed on it.
3. The teacher moves about the room with an electric fan, or students move to the teacher's desk, on which a compass card and a fan are located. They properly describe the direction of wind flow.

Suggested critical thinking questions

Part 1: Wind vane

1. Predict which way the head (paper clip end) of the wind vane will point when the fan is turned on. Was your prediction correct? Why or why not?
2. Explain how the compass card is used to name the direction from which the wind blows.
3. Why does the wind vane direction cause some people to name the blowing wind incorrectly?

Figure 7-3 shows how to assemble the anemometer.

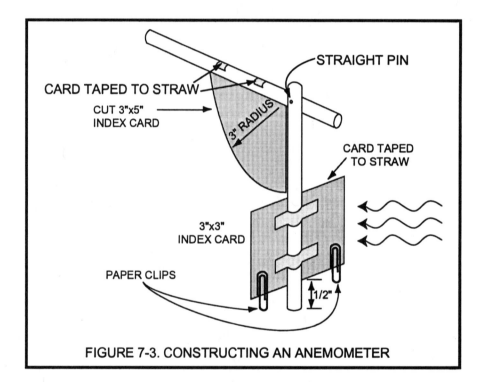

CARD TAPED TO STRAW
CUT 3"x5" INDEX CARD
3" RADIUS
STRAIGHT PIN
CARD TAPED TO STRAW
3"x3" INDEX CARD
PAPER CLIPS
1/2"

FIGURE 7-3. CONSTRUCTING AN ANEMOMETER

Materials

Part 2: Anemometer

Per group of 2 students:

two 8" straws	straight pin
one 3" x 3" index card	marking pen
(cut from a 3" x 5" index card)	cellophane tape
one 3" x 5" index card	scissors & 2 paper clips

Getting started

Part 2: Anemometer

1. The teacher draws a 3″ radius curve using one corner of a 3″ x 5″ index card as the center of the radius.
2. Students cut the quarter circle out of the end.
3. The teacher or the students transfer the wind speed marks to the curve of the index card. To place wind speed marks, measure along the 3″ radius curve a distance of 1½″ for 5 mph, 3″ for 10 mph, and 3¼″ for 15 mph.
4. Students assemble the anemometer as shown in Figure 7-3.
5. Students should listen to weather reports and make a chart of how things (grass, flags, leaves, smoke) react to different wind speeds.

Suggested critical thinking questions

Part 2: Anemometer

1. Predict how the moving arm will behave as the wind speed increases. Was your prediction correct? Why or why not?
2. What would be the effect of adding weight to the bottom of the moving arm? How would this help you measure higher wind speeds?

Figure 7-4 shows how to assemble a rain gauge.

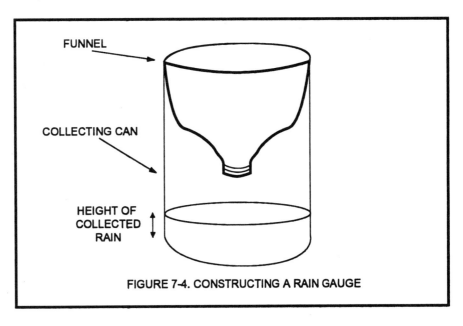

FIGURE 7-4. CONSTRUCTING A RAIN GAUGE

Materials

Part 3: Rain gauge

Per group of 2 students:

> empty can, not more than 3" in diameter, to be used as a collecting can
> funnel made from the top of a 1-liter plastic soda bottle (the funnel should have the same diameter as the can)
> 12" ruler
> 4" high salt shaker filled with water

Getting started

Part 3: Rain gauge

1. The teacher prepares the funnel cut from a plastic soda bottle top (Figure 7-4).
2. Students place the funnel inside the collecting can.
3. Students fill the salt shaker with water and shake it over the funnel to simulate rainfall. When the shaker is empty, the funnel is removed and the amount of rainfall is measured.
4. Students measure the height of the water with the ruler.

Suggested critical thinking questions

Part 3: Rain gauge

1. Why is the daily, seasonal, or yearly rainfall important?
2. In cold weather it sometimes snows. How would you measure the amount of snowfall each day?
3. How would you use your rain gauge to measure the amount of water received in a snowfall?

How are atmospheric moisture and pressure measured?

Background

Air behaves like a sponge, in that it can absorb moisture. Also, the higher the air temperature, the more moisture it can hold. At any given temperature, the amount of moisture in the air can be compared to the maximum it could hold. This is called *relative humidity*. Absolutely dry air has 0% relative humidity. *Saturated* air is carrying its maximum moisture for that air temperature and therefore has 100% relative humidity.

A *psychrometer* is used to measure relative humidity. It has two thermometers. The bulb of one of them is covered by a wet cotton wick. Air blowing over the wick causes evaporation, which lowers the temperature of the thermometer. The difference in air temperature between the two thermometers is used to look up the relative humidity on a chart.

The entire atmosphere is pressing down on the earth. The instrument used to detect changes in atmospheric pressure is called a *barometer*. The atmospheric pressure is equal to an average of 14.7 pounds per square inch at the earth's surface. This is also given as an equivalent millibar pressure of 1013.2 or 29.9 inches of mercury in a *mercurial barometer*. An *aneroid barometer* uses a sealed container of air that expands or contracts as air pressure changes. This movement is shown on a *calibrated* dial.

Air pressure changes slightly as weather systems cross your area. Low-pressure systems usually result from the passage of warm, moist air. In contrast, high-pressure systems usually result from the passage of cool, dry air.

Figure 7-5 shows how to construct a psychrometer. Figure 7-6 is a chart of relative humidity.

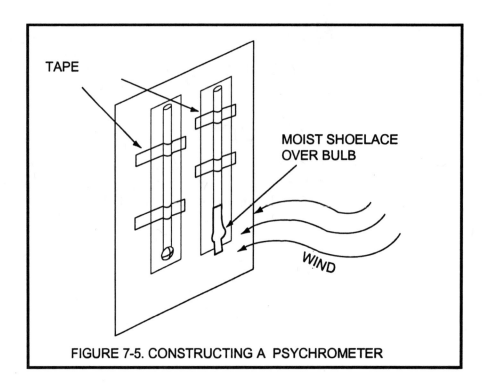

FIGURE 7-5. CONSTRUCTING A PSYCHROMETER

		TEMPERATURE DIFFERENCE BETWEEN DRY BULB AND WET BULB THERMOMETERS (F°)											
	1	**3**	**5**	**7**	**9**	**11**	**13**	**15**	**17**	**19**	**21**	**23**	**25**
30	89	68	47	27	8	0							
35	91	73	52	36	20	4	0						
40	92	76	61	46	31	16	2	0					
45	93	79	65	51	39	26	14	2	0				
50	93	81	68	56	44	33	22	12	2	0			
55	94	82	71	59	49	39	29	20	11	2	0		
60	94	84	73	63	53	44	35	27	18	10	2	0	
65	95	85	75	66	57	48	40	32	25	17	10	3	0
70	95	86	77	68	60	52	44	37	30	23	17	10	4
75	96	87	78	70	63	55	48	41	34	28	22	16	11
80	96	87	79	72	64	57	51	44	38	32	27	21	16
85	96	88	80	73	66	59	52	46	41	35	29	25	20
90	96	89	81	75	68	62	56	50	44	39	34	29	24
95	96	90	82	76	70	64	58	52	46	42	37	32	27
100	96	90	83	77	71	65	59	54	49	44	40	35	31

DRY BULB TEMPERATURE (°F)

FIGURE 7-6. RELATIVE HUMIDITY CHART

Materials

For the entire class:

electric fan

Part 1: Psychrometer

Per group of 4 students:

8½" x 11" cardboard   relative humidity chart
2 calibrated thermometers   (Figure 7-6)
1" shoelace (for wick)   small container of water at
cellophane tape   room temperature

Getting started

Part 1: Psychrometer

1. Students slip a piece of shoelace over one thermometer bulb to make the wet bulb thermometer.
2. Students tape the two thermometers side by side on an 8½" x 11" piece of cardboard.
3. Students wet the shoelace with water at room temperature and hold the thermometers near the fan until the wet bulb temperature stops dropping.
4. Students record both dry bulb and wet bulb temperatures and calculate the difference.
5. Students use the dry bulb temperature and the temperature difference between the dry bulb and wet bulb thermometers to determine the relative humidity from the chart (Figure 7-6).

Suggested critical thinking questions

Part 1: Psychrometer

1. Explain why the shoelace is wetted on the wet bulb thermometer.
2. Predict what will happen to the temperature reading when air blows over the wet bulb thermometer. Was your prediction correct? Why or why not?
3. What is the relation between relative humidity and your comfort? Why?

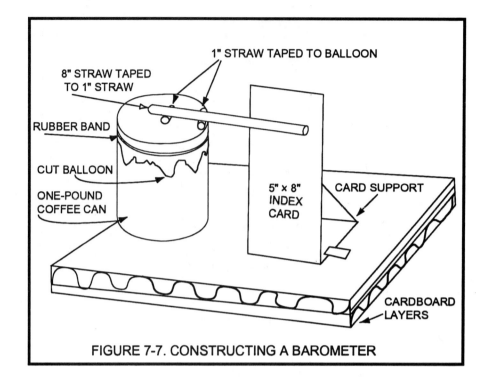

8" STRAW TAPED
TO 1" STRAW

1" STRAW TAPED TO BALLOON

RUBBER BAND

CUT BALLOON

ONE-POUND
COFFEE CAN

5" x 8"
INDEX
CARD

CARD SUPPORT

CARDBOARD
LAYERS

FIGURE 7-7. CONSTRUCTING A BAROMETER

Figure 7-7 shows how to assemble an aneroid barometer.

Materials

Part 2: Aneroid barometer

two 6" x 11" pieces of cardboard
1-lb coffee can
12" round balloon
3" rubber band
8" straw
two 1" pieces of 5" x 8" index card
cellophane tape

Getting started

Part 2: Aneroid barometer

1. Students assemble the aneroid barometer (Figure 7-7) making
    sure that the balloon is split lengthwise and taut over the mouth
    of the can and that the rubber band is reasonably tight.

2. Students listen to a radio or television report of barometric pressure in their local area and mark this reading on the card to the right of the center of the straw.
3. Students should always view the pointer from the same angle to ensure accuracy.
4. Students periodically listen to the radio or television report of barometric pressure and mark the card accordingly.

Suggested critical thinking questions

Part 2: Aneroid barometer

1. Predict what will happen to the diaphragm (balloon) shape as the outside air pressure increases or decreases. Was your prediction correct? Why or why not?
2. How is the position of the long straw affected by changes in the shape of the diaphragm?
3. What weather changes might accompany a rising barometer (increasing barometric pressure)?
4. What weather changes might accompany a falling barometer (decreasing barometric pressure)?
5. How would a change in the temperature of air inside your barometer cause its reading to be less accurate? What would you do to prevent air temperature from changing inside your barometer?

chapter 8

The earth's waters are in constant motion

| *How do rivers start to flow?*

Background

Some rain falls on hilly or mountainous areas. Some of this rain may go back into the air *(evaporate)*, some may sink into the soil, and some may flow on the surface. This flow of water travels down the sides *(slopes)* of the *hills* or *mountains*. Many lines of flow come together to form a *stream* that carries the water further downhill. When many streams come together, they form a *river*, which usually carries the water to the *ocean*.

Figure 8-1 shows a setup for studying the relation of rainfall and streams.

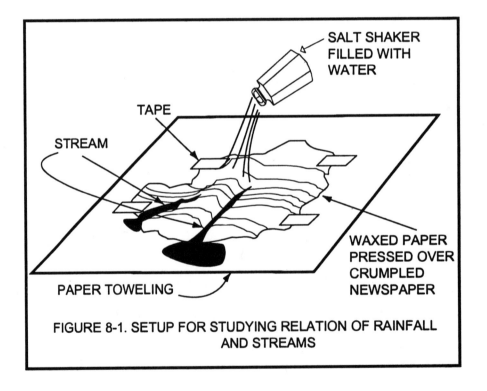

FIGURE 8-1. SETUP FOR STUDYING RELATION OF RAINFALL AND STREAMS

Materials

Per group of 4 students:

1 sheet of crumpled newspaper
12″ x 12″ piece of wax paper
4 sheets of paper toweling (enough to cover a desk)
salt shaker filled with water
cellophane tape

Getting started

1. The teacher covers and tapes paper toweling to students' desks.
2. The teacher places a crumpled and flattened newspaper sheet in center of desk.
3. The teacher flattens waxed paper on top of the crumpled newspaper sheet and tapes it to the paper toweling.
4. Students hold the salt shaker about 6″ above the waxed paper and sprinkle water onto the paper to simulate rain.

Suggested critical thinking questions

1. What do you think will happen to the raindrops at the top of the waxed paper hill?
2. What will happen to the raindrops at the top of the hill when you add more rain to them?
3. What causes the raindrops to move along certain paths? What are such paths called on the earth?
4. Why does more water end up at certain places on the paper toweling? What do we call such places on the earth?

How do water waves begin and end?

Background

Waves form when wind blows over a part of a *lake, ocean,* or large *river.* Stronger winds and larger bodies of water allow the growth of larger waves. Wave motion decreases and ceases when the wave travels far from the wind or when the wave runs up on the shore and loses its energy.

Other waves *(tsunami)* are caused by *earthquakes* or by *meteorites* crashing into the oceans. But these waves are very rare on the coast of the U.S. mainland. *Tidal rise* and fall is also a different type of wave caused by the *gravity* of the moon and the sun.

Figure 8-2 shows a way of simulating the generation of water waves.

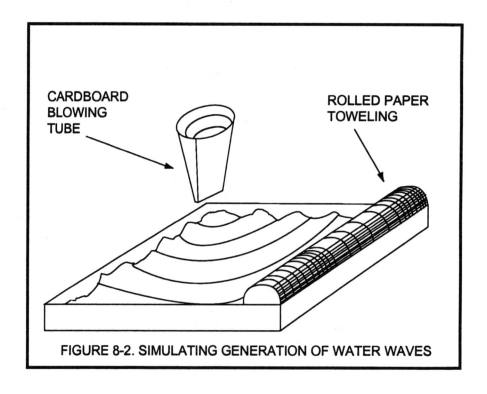

CARDBOARD BLOWING TUBE

ROLLED PAPER TOWELING

FIGURE 8-2. SIMULATING GENERATION OF WATER WAVES

Materials

Per group of 2 students:

> 6″ x 14″ × 2″ tray
> 6″ long cardboard tube
> 4 pieces of paper toweling

Getting started

1. Students fill the tray with 1″ of water.
2. Students roll paper toweling and place it in the narrow back end of the tray.
3. Students squash one end of the cardboard tube and hold the squashed end vertically above the narrow front end of the tray (about 2″ above the water surface).
4. Students blow short bursts of air onto the water surface.

Suggested critical thinking questions

1. How will the water in the tray behave when you blow onto its surface? Was your prediction correct? Why or why not?
2. What happens to the size of the waves if you blow harder? Was your prediction correct? Why or why not?
3. How does the paper toweling at the far end of the tray affect the wave?
4. What will happen to the water surface soon after you stop blowing? Was your prediction correct? Why or why not?
5. What will the waves look like if the near end of the tray is lifted about 1″ and then dropped back onto the desk (table) to simulate an earthquake?
6. How are these waves similar to or different from the wind waves that you made in the tray?

| *What causes ocean currents?*

Background

There are two major types of ocean *currents: surface currents,* which are driven by the wind, and *deep currents,* which result from differences in *density* of ocean water.

In each hemisphere there are bands of wind that blow generally from east to west or from west to east. These are the trade winds, the prevailing westerlies, and the polar easterlies. These winds cause a large area of ocean surface water to move in either a clockwise or a counterclockwise direction.

Cold ocean water is generally denser than warm ocean water. Its density causes it to sink toward the floor of the ocean. It spreads in a north or south direction as a bottom or near-bottom current. Over time, this moving layer of water warms and rises back to the ocean surface. This results in a slow vertical circulation.

Figure 8-3 shows a demonstration of ocean surface currents.

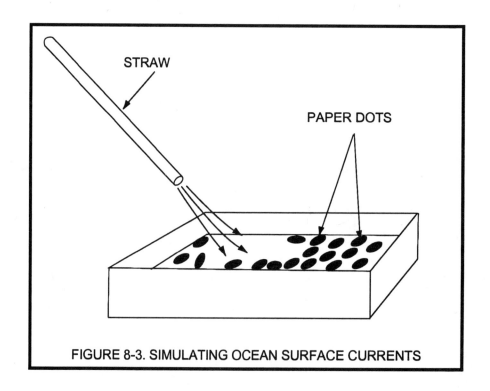

STRAW

PAPER DOTS

FIGURE 8-3. SIMULATING OCEAN SURFACE CURRENTS

Materials

Part 1

Per group of 4 students:

    clear plastic shoebox or aquarium two-thirds filled with water
        at room temperature
    8" straw
    10 paper dots from a hole punch

Getting started

Part 1

1. Student sprinkles paper dots over the water surface.
2. Student blows through the straw to make a slow, deliberate stream of air. The straw should be angled at a near corner of the shoebox and against the side of the box. The end of the straw should be about 1" from the water surface (see Figure 8-3).

Suggested critical thinking questions

Part 1

1. Predict the path of the paper dots as you blow across the water. Was your prediction correct? Why or why not?
2. What is your hypothesis about the effect of the earth's wind bands on ocean surface currents? How do the results of your activity help to prove or disprove your hypothesis?

Figure 8-4 shows a way of simulating formation of ocean bottom currents.

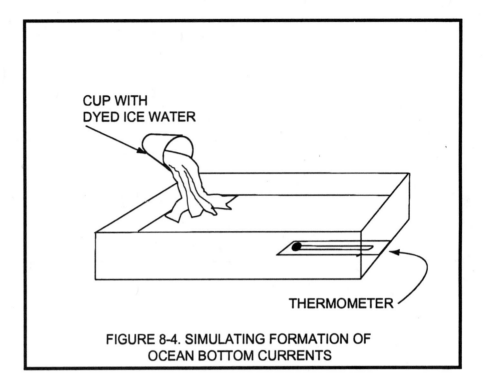

CUP WITH
DYED ICE WATER

THERMOMETER

FIGURE 8-4. SIMULATING FORMATION OF
OCEAN BOTTOM CURRENTS

Materials

Part 2

Per group of 4 students:

> clear plastic shoebox or aquarium (two-thirds filled with water
>   at room temperature)
> 20 drops of red food coloring
> spoon or coffee stirrer
> 2 thermometers
> 8-oz. cup half filled with ice and water
> empty 8-oz. cup

Getting started

Part 2

1. One thermometer is placed on the bottom of the box or
   aquarium near its far end.
2. Unmelted ice should be removed from the ice water cup and
   placed in a sink or in the empty cup.

3. Measure and record the temperature of the ice water.
4. Carefully place 20 drops of food coloring into the ice water and stir.
5. Hold the cup close to the water's surface at the near end of the box or aquarium and slowly pour in the cold, colored water.

Suggested critical thinking questions

Part 2

1. Predict the movement of the dyed cold water as it is poured into the room temperature water of the box or aquarium. Was your prediction correct? Why or why not?
2. How does the difference in temperature of the two water volumes explain the movement of the dyed cold water?
3. Predict how the temperature of water on the bottom of the box or aquarium will be affected by the addition of the dyed cold water? Does the temperature reading support your prediction? Why or why not?
4. What will happen to the color of the entire volume of water over time? What causes this change of color? How do temperature readings at the top and bottom of the water volume help to explain any color change?
5. How might the sinking of cold ocean water around Antarctica and southern Greenland be compared to the movement of the ice water in your activity?

chapter 9

The earth's interior changes result in surface changes: Earthquakes

grades K–2 | *How are buildings affected by earthquakes?*

Background

The earth is made up of many layers of solid or semisolid materials. The earth's outermost layer, called the *lithosphere,* includes the solid *crust* and solid upper *mantle* layers. The lithosphere is broken into many jigsaw-like pieces (see the discussion of plate tectonics in Chapter 10) that are in constant slow motion. This motion may cause the rock to break in a localized area. Such rock breakage causes both surface and internal vibrations, which are called an *earthquake.*

Generally, the closer you are to where an earthquake occurs, the stronger are the ground vibrations. Very strong vibrations can cause buildings to collapse.

Figure 9-1 shows an earthquake vibration device.

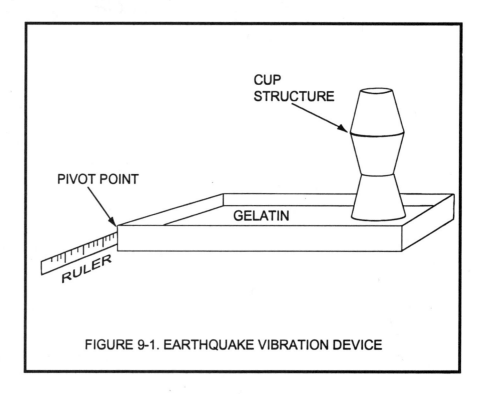

FIGURE 9-1. EARTHQUAKE VIBRATION DEVICE

Materials

Per group of 3 students:

14" x 6" × 2" plastic tray
12" plastic ruler
3 paper cups
cellophane tape
2 packages of flavored gelatin

Getting started

1. One day prior to the activity, the teacher prepares a mixture for each tray by using two packages of flavored gelatin mixed with 5 cups of boiling water.
2. Students invert one paper cup and place it near the end of the tray. They invert the second paper cup and tape it to the third cup. They place these cups on top of the first cup (see Figure 9-1).
3. A student uses the thumb and forefinger of one hand to hold the 2" mark on the ruler against the near edge of the tray. With the other hand, the student vigorously flicks the free end of the ruler.

Suggested critical thinking questions

1. Predict (guess) what will happen to the paper cup structure when the free end of the ruler is flicked. Was your prediction (guess) correct? Why or why not?
2. Describe the motion of the gelatin when the ruler is flicked.
3. How does the motion of the gelatin affect the paper cups?
4. How is the motion of the gelatin and the paper cup structure similar to, or different from, the motion of the ground and buildings during an earthquake?

| *How can we record earthquake waves?*

Background

You probably would not notice the ground shaking if you were thousands of miles away from the *epicenter* of an *earthquake*. However, such ground vibrations could be recorded by sensitive *seismographs* used by scientists *(seismologists)* who study earthquakes. A seismograph instrument has a suspended mass that remains stationary as earthquake waves pass by. The amount of ground motion is recorded on a paper tracing called a *seismogram*. Usually, three directions of ground motion are recorded from separate seismographs: north–south, east–west, and vertical. The seismograph model in your activity records the *amplitude* (amount of ground movement) caused by simulated *earthquake waves*. Only one direction of motion will be recorded by this device. In your model, the marker (attached to the stationary mass) makes a recording of the amount of shaking of the table underneath your setup.

The amplitude of earthquake waves recorded on a seismogram is a measure of the amount of energy released by an earthquake. In 1935, the American seismologist Charles Richter devised a scale to measure the strength of earthquakes on the basis of their seismogram recordings.

Figure 9-2 shows a horizontal seismograph device.

Materials

Per group of 3 students:

    chair whose back is at least 12" above the table
    table/desk
    2 bent wire coat hangers (thick wire)
    masking tape
    small ball of twine
    1 stick of clay
    marking pen
    2 pieces of 8" x 11" graph paper
    wooden block (at least 2" x 4" x 8")

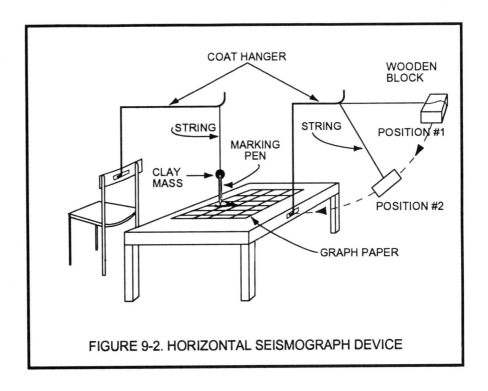

FIGURE 9-2. HORIZONTAL SEISMOGRAPH DEVICE

Getting started

1. Assemble the materials as shown in Figure 9-2.
2. Draw a horizontal line along the middle of the graph paper, and position the line under the marking pen. Make sure the pen is in contact with the graph paper.
3. Keeping the string tight, lift the block so that it is parallel with the table top (position 1 in Figure 9-2). Then, release the block so that it strikes the edge of the table.
4. Replace the graph paper and repeat the procedure, but lift the block only halfway (position 2 in Figure 9-2).

Suggested critical thinking questions

1. Predict what the pen mark on the graph paper will look like when the wooden block strikes the edge of the table from position 1. Was your prediction correct? Why or why not?
2. Predict the result when the block of wood is lifted only halfway and released (position 2 in Figure 9-2). Was your prediction correct? Why or why not?
3. Compare and contrast the recordings on the graph paper. What is the relationship between the amount of energy released by dropping the block from different heights and the distance over which the marking pen moved?
4. How are your seismograph and seismograms similar to or different from those used by seismologists?

| *Why do earthquakes cause some buildings to tilt or sink?*

Background

Liquefaction is the quicksand-like behavior of *sediment* being shaken by earthquake waves. Liquefaction happens because groundwater is forced up, lubricates soil particles, and allows them to flow past each other easily. Such soil particles can no longer support the mass of structures like buildings and bridges. Such structures tilt, sink, or collapse into the liquefied sediment.

The type of soil and rock underlying an area determines how much shaking will occur as earthquake waves pass by. At the same distance from an earthquake, soil will shake more than rock layers. Therefore, human sensation and building damage in an earthquake are directly related to the geology of an area. A qualitative scale that describes the behavior of humans and structures during an earthquake was devised by Mercalli in 1902 and modified in 1931.

Figure 9-3 shows a simplified Mercalli intensity scale. Figure 9-4 is a diagram of a liquefaction device.

Materials

Per group of 3 students:

> 14" x 3" x 2" plastic tray
> 2 lb. of potting soil
> 6 large zinc-plated washers (½" inside diameter)
> 1-liter container of water

Getting started

1. Fill the tray halfway with a smoothed layer of potting soil. *Do not* compact the soil.
2. Gently pour water into the near end of the tray until a thin film of water covers the entire soil surface.
3. Sprinkle an additional ¼" of potting soil over the entire surface of the tray, and gently smooth it.

INTENSITY	WHAT PEOPLE FEEL	HOW OBJECTS AND BUILDINGS ARE AFFECTED
I	Not felt	No damage
II	Slight shock felt by people in bed on upper floors	No damage
III	Minor vibrations felt indoors	No damage
IV	Medium vibrations felt indoors	Windows and doors rattle, chandeliers swing, plaster may crack.
V	Felt indoors, strong vibrations indoors, sleepers awakened	Doors swing, objects fall, walls crack.
VI	Very strong vibrations felt by everyone, frightened people run outdoors, walking is unsteady.	Adobe and weak masonry show slight cracks.
VII	Extreme vibrations make standing difficult, automobile drivers notice vibrations	Building stones fall and weak buildings show larger cracks.
VIII	Steering automobiles is difficult	Some damage to reinforced masonry, weaker buildings seriously damaged, twisting and collapse of towers and chimneys.
IX	General panic	Serious damage to reinforced masonry, weaker buildings destroyed, serious damage to reservoirs, underground pipes are broken, ground cracks, and soil liquefies.
X	Many deaths and injuries	Most masonry and frame structures destroyed, ground badly cracked, train tracks bent, landslides on steep slopes and riverbanks.
XI	Many deaths and injuries	Few masonry or frame structures remain standing, train tracks show major bends, underground pipelines out of service.
XII	Many deaths and injuries	Nearly total damage, large rock masses are shifted, objects are thrown into the air.

FIGURE 9-3.   SIMPLIFIED MERCALLI INTENSITY SCALE

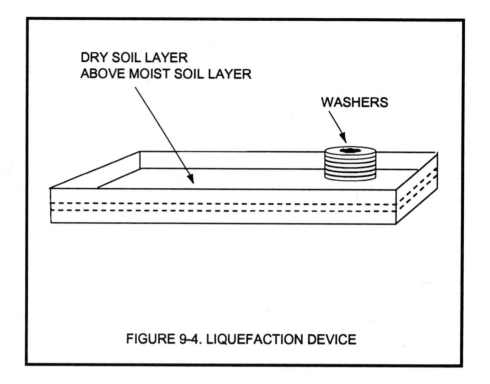

DRY SOIL LAYER
ABOVE MOIST SOIL LAYER

WASHERS

FIGURE 9-4. LIQUEFACTION DEVICE

4. Gently place a stack of 6 washers on the soil surface about 1″ from the far end of the tray.
5. Tap the near end of the tray repeatedly with your fingertips.

Suggested critical thinking questions

1. Predict what will happen to the washers when they are placed gently on the soil surface. Was your prediction correct? Why or why not?
2. Predict what will happen to the soil and the stack of washers after about one minute of tapping. Was your prediction correct? Why or why not?
3. What caused the motion of the washers?
4. How is the behavior of the washers similar to that of buildings constructed on sediment layers?
5. What Mercalli Scale number would describe the behavior of the washers (Figure 9-3)?
6. Design a building that could resist the movements resulting from soil liquefaction.

chapter 10

The constant motion of lithospheric plates causes folding, faulting, and mountain building

| *How are landforms the same or different?*

Background

Geologists believe that the earth's surface is as varied today as it has ever been. There are very high *mountains*, like the Rocky Mountains of the western United States, and deep river *valleys*, like the Grand Canyon. Other major types of surface features are the large *plateaus* and relatively flat *plains*.

Most of us live in communities where there is little difference in the height *(elevation)* of surface features. However, in many areas there are *hills, stream valleys,* and *lake* or *ocean shorelines* that form the uphill and downhill surface features.

Figure 10-1 shows some types of landforms.

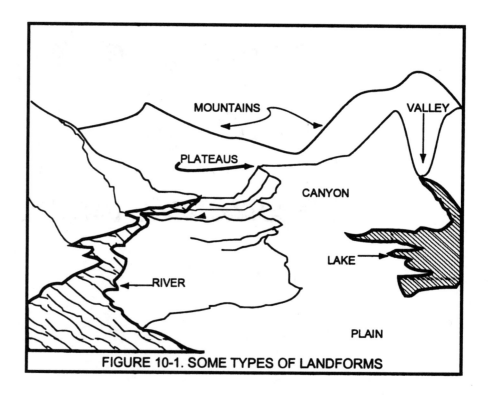

FIGURE 10-1. SOME TYPES OF LANDFORMS

Materials

Per group of 2 students:

pictures of the earth's major surface features
sand table or the equivalent
shoebox
glue
scissors

Getting started

1. The teacher collects, or asks students to bring to class, pictures of surface features.
2. Students classify pictures according to shared properties of the surface features.
3. Students construct dioramas or collages to show relationships between types of surface features and adaptation of people to the environment around each feature (clothing, housing, food supply, and transportation).
4. Students use the sand table or its equivalent to construct a model of the types of earth surface features.

Suggested critical thinking questions

1. Explain the groupings of pictures of the earth's surface features.
2. From the picture groupings, describe what is the same or different about the mountains, hills, valleys, plateaus, and plains.
3. Describe the earth features found in the neighborhood or community.
4. How do the earth's surface features determine which animals might be found in an area shown by a particular picture grouping?
5. What clothing would people wear in an area shown by a particular picture grouping?
6. Were you able to include all types of earth surface features in your sand table model? Why or why not?

Background

Much of the earth's land surface is covered by soil. In many places, layered rock lies beneath the soil. Such rock layers can be moved by internal stresses in the earth. The rocks can bend *(fold)* or break *(fault)* when stress is directed horizontally (parallel to the earth's surface). Rocks that are folded form a series of up folds *(anticlines)* and down folds *(synclines)* that look like waves on the ocean (Figure 10-2). Instead of folding, the rocks may break and form *thrust faults* (Figure 10-3), which shove a rock layer (or rock layers) on top of neighboring rock layers. Or the rock layers may form *lateral faults* that allow one part of the rock layer to slip past the opposite part (Figure 10-4).

When the stress is directed vertically the rock layers tend to break. Such a break *(gravity fault)* causes one side of the rock layer to move up or down in relation to its neighboring rock (Figure 10-5).

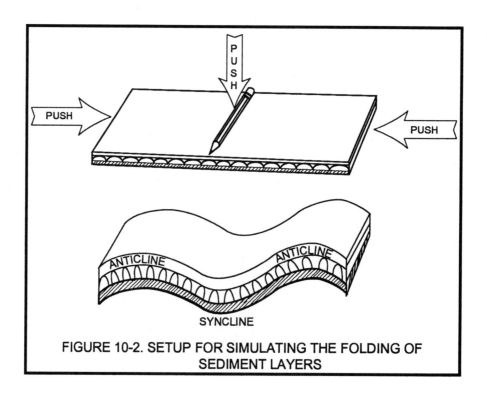

FIGURE 10-2. SETUP FOR SIMULATING THE FOLDING OF SEDIMENT LAYERS

Materials

Part 1: Folding

Per group of 4 students:

> stack of 15 sheets of multicolored construction paper
> one pencil
> a picture of folded mountains

Getting started

Part 1: Folding

1. Students place a stack of construction paper on the table top.
2. A student places a pencil on the top of the stack halfway between the ends (Figure 10-2) and holds it in place.
3. The second and third students push, simultaneously, from both ends of the paper stack toward the pencil.

Suggested critical thinking questions

1. Predict what type of landform will be created when the ends of the paper stack are pushed toward the pencil. Draw what you think the layers will look like.
2. What do you think is the cause of folded mountains on earth?
3. How are the folded mountains made in your activity with the paper stack similar to or different from the folded mountains shown in the picture?

Materials

Part 2: Thrust faulting

For use with the whole class:

> 12" x 12" x 2" baking pan

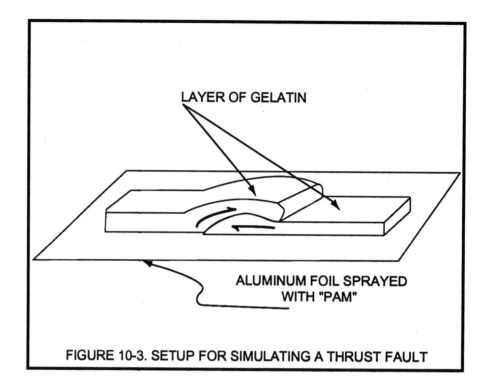

LAYER OF GELATIN

ALUMINUM FOIL SPRAYED
WITH "PAM"

FIGURE 10-3. SETUP FOR SIMULATING A THRUST FAULT

Per group of 4 students:

8" x 8" x 2" baking pan
4 packages of gelatin (flavored)
2 cups of water
can of Pam or other nonstick vegetable cooking spray
12" x 12" sheet of aluminum foil

Getting started

Part 2: Thrust faulting

1. The teacher prepares gelatin 24 hours in advance (using half the water called for in the package directions).
2. The teacher warms the bottom of the 8" x 8" baking pan by placing it, for about 10 seconds, into a larger pan filled with 1" of very warm water.
3. The teacher flips the gelatin onto the aluminum foil and cuts the gelatin into 4" squares (2 squares for each team of 2 students).
4. Students spray nonstick coating liquid onto 12" x 12" sheets of aluminum foil.

5. Students place gelatin squares next to each other on the foil and spray both inside edges of the gelatin with nonstick coating liquid.
6. Students push one gelatin square against the other square.

Suggested critical thinking questions

1. Predict what will happen when the two gelatin squares are pushed against each other. Did the gelatin behave as predicted? Why or why not?
2. If two continents on lithospheric plates were being pushed together, in the same manner as the gelatin, what might happen?

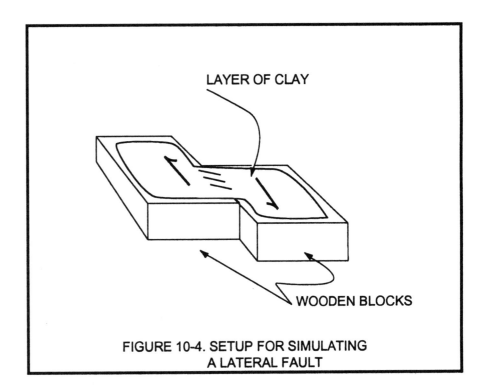

FIGURE 10-4. SETUP FOR SIMULATING
A LATERAL FAULT

Materials

Part 3: Lateral faulting

Per group of 2 students:

stick of modeling clay
two 2" x 6" x 1" wooden blocks

Getting started

Part 3: Lateral faulting

1. One student holds the long edges of the blocks together.
2. The second student flattens the stick of clay onto both blocks, making a clay layer that is about $^1/_8$" thick and making sure that it sticks to the top surfaces of both blocks.
3. One student holds one block in position while the second student slides the second block slowly past it.

Suggested critical thinking questions

1. Predict what will happen to the clay layer as one block slides past the other. Did the clay layer behave as predicted? Why or why not?
2. If two lithospheric plates were sliding past each other in the same manner as the blocks, what might happen?
3. Compare and contrast the fault in the clay with the San Andreas and similar faults in California.

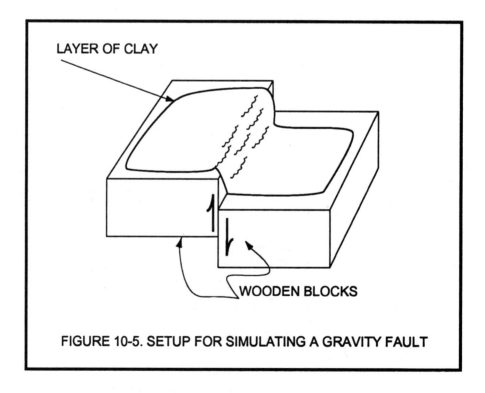

FIGURE 10-5. SETUP FOR SIMULATING A GRAVITY FAULT

Materials

Part 4: Gravity faulting

Per group of 2 students:

> stick of modeling clay
> two 2" x 6" x 1" wooden blocks

Getting started

Part 4: Gravity faulting

1. One student holds the long edges of the blocks together.
2. The second student flattens the stick of clay onto both blocks, making the clay layer about $^1/_8''$ thick and making sure that it sticks to the surface of both blocks.
3. One student holds one block in position while the second student slowly lifts the second block.

Suggested critical thinking questions

1. Predict what will happen to the clay as one block is slowly lifted past the other. Did the clay behave as predicted? Why or why not?
2. If there was vertical stress on one portion of a lithospheric plate, what might happen?

Why do mountains form where lithospheric plates collide?

Background

The building of mountains, except for volcanic mountains, takes place through a combination of folding and faulting motions. The stresses that cause such activity result from collision of the jigsaw-like *lithospheric plates*. The lithospheric plates are undergoing a slow movement caused by *plate-tectonic* forces that are not yet understood by *geologists*. The plates are composed of continental lithosphere, ocean lithosphere, or a combination of both. The leading edge of a plate will be destroyed as it sinks into the *mantle* at a *trench*. This plate motion is known as *subduction*. At the same time, the opposite plate edge is being added to by *volcanoes* or *lava extrusion* along a portion of the *mid-ocean ridge*. The sinking and melting of the leading edge of a plate and its replacement at the mid-ocean ridge represents a recycling of lithosphere materials over millions of years.

Not all of the seafloor rocks and sediments are subducted into a trench. Some are plastered onto the tectonic plate that is landward of the trench. Also, these rocks and sediments may be squeezed between opposing masses of continental lithosphere to form folded and faulted mountains like the Appalachians and the Himalayas.

Figure 10-6 illustrates subduction.

Materials

Per group of 4 students:

> 8½" x 15" piece of corrugated cardboard
> 30" piece of adding machine tape
> two 1" x 3" x ¾" wooden blocks
> 3" x 6" strip of folded paper napkin cut lengthwise (same width as the adding machine tape)
> cellophane tape
> 3 large bobby pins

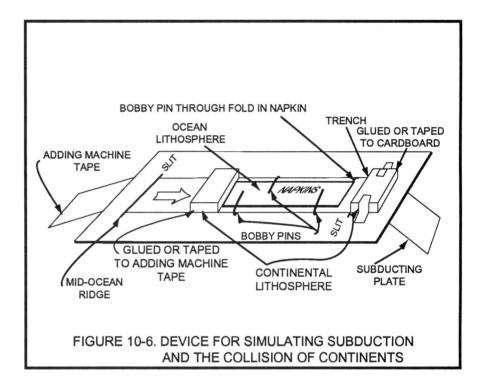

FIGURE 10-6. DEVICE FOR SIMULATING SUBDUCTION
AND THE COLLISION OF CONTINENTS

Getting started

1. Prior to distributing materials, the teacher uses a serrated-edge knife to cut 3" slits in the cardboards. Each slit should be parallel to and 2" from the narrow ends of the cardboard.
2. Students cut a paper napkin into a strip of the same width as the adding machine tape.
3. Students assemble the subduction "machine" as shown in Figure 10-6 and label the mid-ocean ridge, trench, ocean lithosphere, continental lithosphere, and subducting plate. (Make sure that the last bobby pin is through the folds in the napkin strip.)
4. When the subduction "machine" is assembled, one student will hold the cardboard and a second student will pull the adding machine tape, representing the subducting plate, downward at a 45-degree angle until folds have formed in the napkin.

Suggested critical thinking questions

1. Predict what will happen to the napkin as the adding machine tape is pulled downward. Was your prediction correct? Why or why not?
2. Compare and contrast the behavior of the napkin with the behavior of rocks caught between continents in collision.
3. Explain the role of the mid-ocean ridges and trenches in the formation and destruction of lithospheric plates.
4. How might plates have moved to create the Appalachian and Himalayan mountain ranges?

chapter 11

Fossils provide evidence of earlier life on earth

How did dinosaurs differ from each other?

Background

Dinosaurs originated long after simple life forms occupied the lands and seas. But they died out (became *extinct*) long before people appeared. Other forms of life survived whatever earth crisis caused the extinction of the dinosaurs.

During the time of dinosaurs, the continents were not of the same shape or in the same place as at present. Dinosaurs lived only in the swamps, forest, and warm waters of these ancient continents. Some dinosaurs were plant eaters and others were flesh eaters. Observing and comparing the characteristics of different dinosaurs help us to understand where they lived, how they moved, and what they ate.

Figure 11-1 provides a chart for dinosaur classification.

DINOSAUR NAME	HOW IT MOVED (LOCOMOTION)	ENVIRONMENT WHERE IT LIVED	TYPE OF FOOD THAT IT ATE

FIGURE 11-1. CHART FOR DINOSAUR CLASSIFICATION

Materials

Per group of 4–6 students:

> models of land- and sea-dwelling dinosaurs (to scale if possible)
> set of pictures of the common dinosaurs
> 8′ length of craft paper
> assorted watercolor paints and brushes
> newspaper for stuffing
> scissors
> staplers

Getting started

1. The teacher completes the chart in Figure 11-1 together with the class, on the basis of students' observations about the dinosaur models.
2. Each student group should select a dinosaur from a different environment and draw a much larger version of it on half the length of the craft paper.
3. Students cut out the figure and then trace it onto the second half of the craft paper.
4. Students cut out the second shape and staple the two together while stuffing the figure with crumpled newspaper sheets.
5. Students paint the dinosaur model. Then each student group gives a talk about its dinosaur.

Suggested critical thinking questions

1. What part or parts of a dinosaur might help you to decide how different dinosaurs moved? Why did you make this choice?
2. What part or parts of a dinosaur help you to decide where it lived? Why did you make this choice?
3. What part or parts of a dinosaur help you decide what kind of food it ate? Why did you make this choice?
4. Why do you think that some dinosaurs had tails, long necks, claws, armor plate, or horns?

Background

Fortunately, extinct life forms often leave remains such as bones or imprints (leaf impressions, footprints) that reveal their existence. These are called *fossils*.

Fossils usually form when animals die and their hard parts are covered by lake, river, or ocean *sediment*. Over millions of years, the sediment turns to rock. Plants usually lack hard parts and are found as *imprints* or outlines. Sometimes, however, the woody parts of plants may be replaced by *minerals* in the *groundwater*. Such fossils are found as *petrified wood*. In the same way, hard parts of animals (bones, eggs, etc.) also may be replaced by minerals in the groundwater.

Scientists who search for the remains of early life forms are called *paleontologists*. They use a variety of tools to remove fossils carefully from the surrounding rock.

Figure 11-2 shows a setup for simulating a fossil dig.

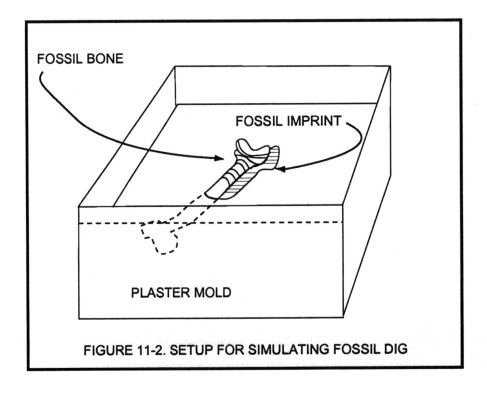

FOSSIL BONE

FOSSIL IMPRINT

PLASTER MOLD

FIGURE 11-2. SETUP FOR SIMULATING FOSSIL DIG

Materials

Per group of 2 students:

> 12 oz. (by volume) plaster of Paris
> 4 oz. (by volume) play sand
> measuring cup
> plastic container (½-pound size)
> plastic container (1-pound size) or small plastic pail
> petroleum jelly
> small chicken or turkey bone
> popsicle stick (or metal spoon)
> plastic knife
> sandwich toothpick
> 3" x 12" strip of paper toweling

Getting started

1. The teacher coats the bones with a thin layer of petroleum jelly.
2. The teacher puts 12 ounces of plaster of Paris into each one-pound plastic container, then stirs and mixes 4–5 oz. of warm water with the plaster. (The mixture should be as thick as pancake batter.)
3. The teacher then slowly stirs and mixes 4 oz. of sand into the plaster of Paris.
4. The teacher pours the plaster mix into each of the smaller plastic containers. Then, out of view of the students, the teacher inserts a bone sideways into the plaster so that a small portion of the end of the bone is still exposed.
5. The teacher sets the containers aside to harden for about 24 hours and places one end of the paper toweling strip on the plaster surface. (The other end should hang over the edge of the container to act as a wick to draw off excess water.)
6. Students should cover the work area with layers of newspaper.
7. Students should invert the container and gently press down until the plaster is released.
8. Students should use a plastic knife or sandwich toothpick to remove the hardened plaster-and-sand mixture slowly from around the top side of the bone.
9. Students should remove the exposed bone to reveal the imprint (mold) of the lower half of the bone.

Suggested critical thinking questions

1. Explain how dinosaur bones ended up in rock layers and became fossils.
2. Describe the relationship between the imprint in the plaster-and-sand mixture and the original bone.
3. If you were a paleontologist who found bones from one dinosaur, what would you do to find out what the whole animal looked like?
4. Which early life forms have been identified by digging of fossils?
5. How would future paleontologists know which life forms shared the earth with us?

grades 5–6 | *How is the age of a fossil related to the rock layer in which it is found?*

Background

A series of *sedimentary rock* layers may be deposited in basins that form where the earth's *lithosphere* is sinking. The earth's lithosphere has sunk to form such *basins* at many places over time. Sometimes the basins are covered by large fresh water lakes and sometimes by shallow ocean water. At other times the basins may dry up.

Animals and plants that die will be buried or washed into the sediment in the basins. As the basin sinks and new sedimentary layers form, the remains of animals and plants that lived in earlier times will be covered by sedimentary layers that contain the remains of later animals and plants. Therefore, under ordinary circumstances, the fossils found in deeper sedimentary layers are older than those found closer to the surface.

Figure 11-3 shows a setup for simulating fossil-bearing sedimentary rock layers.

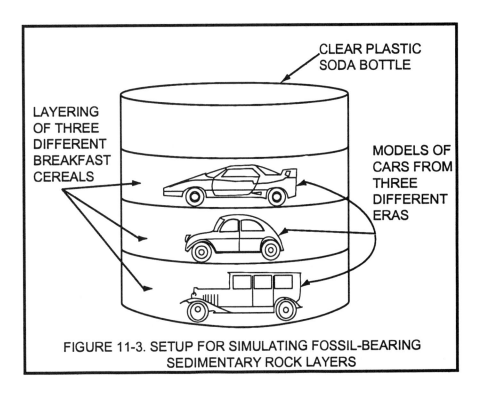

FIGURE 11-3. SETUP FOR SIMULATING FOSSIL-BEARING
SEDIMENTARY ROCK LAYERS

117

Materials

Per group of 2 students:

> 1-liter soda bottle cut off 7½" above its base (at top of label)
> 3 different kinds of dry breakfast cereal
> 3 small automobile models from three distinct stylistic eras
> plastic spoon

Getting started

1. The teacher prepares the soda bottle, pours the lower layer of sediment (breakfast cereal), and places the "oldest" automobile in the cereal against the inside of the soda bottle. The second layer, with the vehicle of intermediate age, and third layer of cereal, with the "youngest" automobile, are placed in the same way.
2. Students spoon out the top layer, recover the automobile, and describe it on a copy of the table (Figure 11-4).
3. Students use the characteristics of each automobile to estimate how long ago such a vehicle was being used.
4. Students repeat the procedure for the middle and bottom layers.
5. Students use library resources to confirm age estimates for the automobiles.

SEDIMENTARY ROCK LAYER	CHARACTERISTICS OF "FOSSIL" (VEHICLE)	ESTIMATED AGE OF "FOSSIL" (VEHICLE)
TOP		
MIDDLE		
BOTTOM		

FIGURE 11-4   DATA SHEET FOR SIMULATED FOSSIL "DIG"

Suggested critical thinking questions

1. What properties of rocks are being simulated by the different cereals in the soda bottle?
2. Which layer of "sediment" (cereal) was the first to be deposited in the container? What is the evidence?
3. What are the "age" relationships among the three "sediment" layers in the container?
4. In nature, what would be the relationship between the age of the sediment layer and the fossils found in it?
5. Suppose you cannot find in your books anything that looks exactly like one of your automobiles. How would similar characteristics of other automobiles help to determine its age? How would paleontologists identify and find the age of the fossil remains of an animal that had not been discovered before?
6. Because paleontologists find many ancient fossils in surface rocks, what must have happened to the younger rocks that once covered these fossils?

chapter 12

Weathering, erosion, and deposition are constantly changing the land surface

How does the wind change landforms?

Background

Strong winds can lift soil and sand particles and carry them to distant locations. The place where the soil and sand have been picked up is *eroded (erosion process)*. The soil and sand particles no longer can be carried when the wind slows. They are *deposited* and build up the land surface *(deposition process)*.

When wind-blown sand is deposited in interior desert regions or beaches, it may pile up into forms called *dunes*.

Figure 12-1 shows a setup for simulating dune formation.

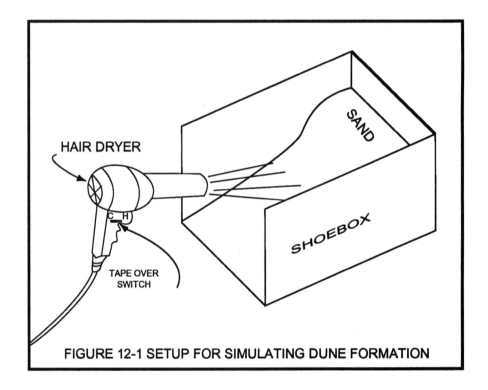

FIGURE 12-1 SETUP FOR SIMULATING DUNE FORMATION

Materials

Per group of 4 students:

shoebox with one narrow end removed
play sand sufficient to make a thin layer on the bottom of the
shoebox

hand-held hair dryer
masking tape
marking pen or crayon
safety goggles

Getting started

Safety hints:

1. *The teacher should plug in and unplug the hair dryers for the students.*
2. *The teacher should tape over the heat control button of the dryer so that only cold air blows.*
3. *The teacher should orient all student activity stations and position students so that sand cannot blow toward the students. Students should wear safety goggles.*

---

1. The teacher places and smoothes the layer of sand on the bottom of each shoebox.
2. The teacher experiments to determine how close the dryer must be to the open end of the shoebox in order for the sand to begin moving.
3. The teacher places a line of masking tape at each station to show where the blower end of the dryer should be placed.
4. Students mark the top level of the sand around the inside of the shoebox.
5. Students turn on the blower and cause sand to move from the open end of the box toward the back

Suggested critical thinking questions

1. What will happen to the level of the sand near the open end of the shoebox when the blower is turned on? Was your prediction (guess) correct? Why or why not?
2. Predict (guess) what will happen to the level of sand at the back end of the shoebox? Was your prediction (guess) correct? Why or why not?
3. How might a farmer try to prevent soil from being blown away by the wind? How can the shoebox and sand be used to test your idea?
4. How might sand fences and dune grass affect the movement of sand on a wind-swept beach?

| *How does water dissolve rock?*

Background

Some gases combine with water in the atmosphere to form weak *acids*. These acids reach the earth during rains. Some rocks will begin to dissolve rapidly when rain falls on them; this is called *chemical weathering*.

The rocks most easily dissolved are *chalk, limestone,* and *marble,* because they are made of a substance *(calcium carbonate)* that changes in the presence of the weak acids. *Caverns* will form as rainwater passes through rocks of this type that lie below the earth's surface.

Figure 12-2 shows a setup for simulation chemical weathering of rocks.

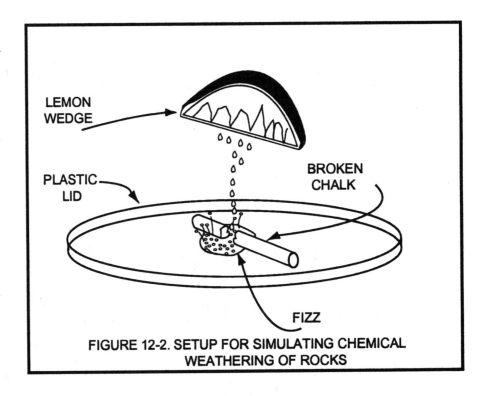

LEMON WEDGE

PLASTIC LID

BROKEN CHALK

FIZZ

FIGURE 12-2. SETUP FOR SIMULATING CHEMICAL WEATHERING OF ROCKS

Materials

Per group of 2 students:

> wedge of lemon or concentrated lemon juice
> seashell or small pieces of chalk
> dish or plastic lid
> blue litmus paper (turns red in the presence of an acid)

Getting started

1. Students should use blue litmus paper to test a drop of lemon juice for the presence of an acid. (The lemon wedges represent rain clouds that are ready to drop rain on the land surface.)
2. Students place the shell or chalk on the dish or lid and slowly squeeze the lemon wedge (cloud) so that drops fall on it.
3. Students should observe small bubbles around the shell or chalk as the "acid rain" falls on it.

Suggested critical thinking questions

1. Predict what will happen when the lemon juice drops fall on the shell or chalk. Was your prediction correct? Why or why not?
2. Predict how the shell or chalk would change if lemon juice were to fall on it for a long time.
3. How can the reaction of rocks to rain be compared to the reaction of the shell or chalk to the lemon juice?
4. What might happen to a marble statue left out in the rain? Explain.

Background

Glaciers covered large parts of northern North America and northern Eurasia up until thousands of years ago. Such glacial ice masses are called *ice caps.* In mountainous regions, individual ice masses flowed down preexisting *river valleys.* These are called *valley glaciers.*

Over time, snow falling in mountain areas is compacted into *glacial ice.* This ice can flow downhill when it builds up into a thick layer. As with the flow of water in a stream, the center of the glacier flows faster than at its sides or base.

Glaciers carry rock debris that erodes the sides and floor of V-shaped river valleys and changes them into broader U-shaped glacial valleys. Polishing and gouging of the exposed rock valley walls and floor by glacier rock debris is evidence that the glacier pushes the debris. Also, the glacial ice carries rock debris in a type of movement similar to a conveyor belt. This debris is then deposited as a ridge of *terminal moraine* at the *snout* (downhill end) of the glacier.

Figure 12-3 shows a setup for simulating the flow of mountain glaciers.

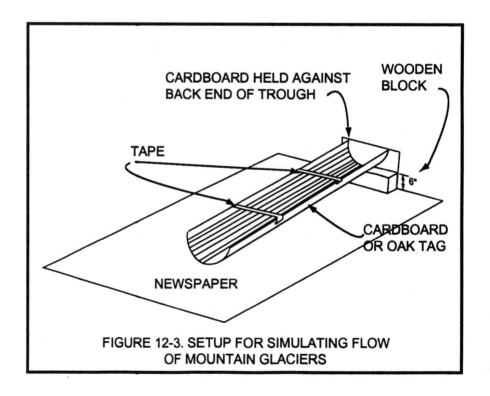

FIGURE 12-3. SETUP FOR SIMULATING FLOW OF MOUNTAIN GLACIERS

Materials

Per group of 4–6 students:

    4" x 4" piece of cardboard
    8½" x 18" cardboard or oak tag
    2 packages of cooked chocolate or vanilla pudding
    cellophane tape
    peanuts
    2 toothpicks broken in half
    6" length of wooden 2" x 6" board
    newspaper to cover table

Getting started

1. The teacher prepares two packages of pudding about 24 hours in advance of class for each student team.
2. Students assemble the apparatus shown in Figure 12-3.
3. With the trough lying flat on the table, students pour the pudding into the rear (closed end) of the trough.
4. Students stick four halves of the toothpicks into the front of the pudding in a straight line across the trough.
5. Students sprinkle about 6 peanuts on the front top of the pudding and spread out an additional 6 peanuts slightly in front of the pudding.
6. Students raise and hold the back end of the trough on the 6" high block of wood.

Suggested critical thinking questions

1. What do you think will happen to the alignment of the toothpicks when the pudding glacier begins to flow? What will this tell you about how fast different parts of the glacier flow?
2. Predict what will happen to the peanuts on top of the glacier. Was your prediction correct? Why or why not?
3. Predict what will happen to the peanuts in front of the glacier. Was your prediction correct? Why or why not?
4. If the peanuts were rocks in a real glacier, what evidence of their movement would be left in the glacial valley?
5. How is the deposit of glacier pudding (at the end of the trough) similar to the mound of sediment (terminal moraine) found at the moving end of a real valley glacier?

chapter 13

Humans can affect the quality of the earth's soil, air, and water

| ## *What makes soil better for plant growth?*

Background

Over thousands of years, rocks break up into smaller particles such as *gravel, sand, silt,* and *clay*. These materials make a thin cover of *sediment* on the earth's land surface. Eventually, decaying plant and animal matter *(humus)* mixes with the small particles of sediment to help plants grow. The mixture of sediment and humus is called *soil*. Ideal soil contains a variety of sizes of rock particles and lots of humus. An adequate supply of rainfall is needed to support plant growth in any soil.

Figure 13-1 shows a setup for the plant growth test.

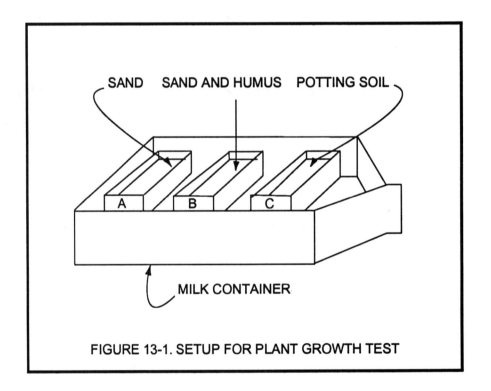

FIGURE 13-1. SETUP FOR PLANT GROWTH TEST

Materials

Per group of 3 students:

3 pint-size milk containers
one 2-liter milk or juice container
6 lima beans (presoaked for 24 hours)
masking tape
8 oz. of play sand
8 oz. of play sand with finely shredded leaves and twigs (or
    play sand and peat moss)
8 oz. of potting soil
spoon or scoop
8 oz. cup
3 hand lenses
scissors
several lengths of yarn

Getting started

Part 1

1. Students place one spoonful of each of the three types of material (growing medium) on a piece of paper and spread it out. They then use the hand lenses to identify the composition of each material.
2. Students return the materials to their original containers.

Suggested critical thinking questions

Part 1

1. Describe the differences among the three different soil materials.
2. Where do you think the different parts of the soil materials came from?

Getting started

Part 2

1. The teacher cuts the 2-liter milk or juice containers in half lengthwise and staples or tapes the spout ends. This will make a tray for the pint containers for each student group.
2. The teacher will prepare enough sand and humus mixture for the entire class.
3. Students should make labels to identify the type of soil material that will be placed in each container.
4. Students will use a pencil to poke three drainage holes into the bottom of each pint container.
5. Students will fill one pint container with sand, one with sand and humus, and one with potting soil. Students should press the materials down lightly so that each container is filled to the same level.
6. Students will label the tray with their names. Then they will place the pint containers in the tray and put ½ cup of tap water in each.
7. After the water has settled, two lima beans should be pushed about 1" deep into each container and covered with the material in the container.
8. Trays should be placed on a windowsill or other sunlight area. After about 48 hours, seeds will begin to germinate.
9. If the students choose to measure the height of the plants as an indicator of growth, then, after an additional 48 hours, students should cut off pieces of the wool yarn to represent height of the bean plants in each container. These should be pasted next to each other on paper or cardboard to show the relative height of each plant. The same procedure should be repeated every 48 hours (where possible) and the new growth in each container compared with previous measurements.
10. Students should add ¼ cup of water to each container every 2 days.

Suggested critical thinking questions

Part 2

1. Which container do you think will have the tallest plants after two weeks of growth? What are your reasons?

2. Explain how you can measure the growth of the plants in each container.

3. Why is it important to add the same amount of water to each container and to give the plants in each container the same amount of sunlight?

4. In your activity, which of the following plant needs (water, sun, soil type) seems to be the reason for the differences in plant growth? Explain your conclusion.

5. What do you think would happen to our food supply if the "good" soil were washed away in floods or blown away in windstorms?

6. What might happen to plant growth if the same soil is used to grow the same vegetables over and over again?

Background

We live in the ocean of air surrounding the earth. The air around us carries many different particles that result from human and plant activities and earth disturbances. Humans contribute to air pollution when they burn vegetation, use fossil fuels, mismanage soil resources, and fail to control industrial smokestack discharges *(emissions)*. In spring and summer, plant *pollen* carried by the wind affects people with *allergies*. Volcanic eruptions shoot dust clouds high into the atmosphere, where they may circle the earth for years as the dust slowly falls back to the earth's surface. Natural fires caused by lightning also contribute to the smoke particles in the atmosphere.

The environmental agencies of federal and state governments and of each major city monitor air quality on a daily basis. They measure dust, *soot,* and pollen carried by winds. They use advanced technology for their measurements, but we can detect airborne particles with simple devices.

Figure 13-2 shows a setup for collecting air particles.

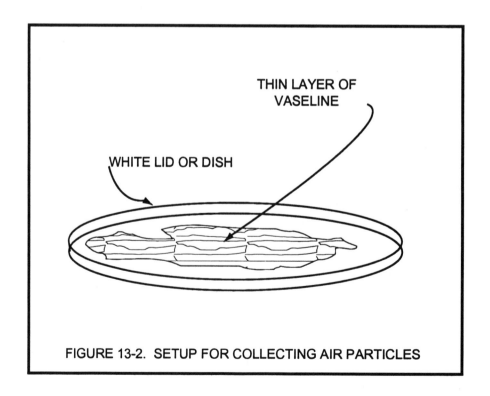

THIN LAYER OF VASELINE

WHITE LID OR DISH

FIGURE 13-2. SETUP FOR COLLECTING AIR PARTICLES

Materials

Per group of 2 students:

8 white plastic or metal lids
teaspoon of petroleum jelly
hand lens
4 plastic zip-lock bags
masking tape

Getting started

1. Students label the back of each lid and examine the lids for cleanliness.
2. Students spread a thin layer of petroleum jelly on the inside of each lid.
3. Students seal four of the lids in the zip-lock bags.
4. Students place one lid on a school windowsill facing traffic and one on a windowsill away from traffic. Students record the lid numbers and locations in their laboratory notebooks.
5. Students place one lid on a windowsill on the windy side of the building and one on the opposite side of the building. (If step 5 locations correspond with step 4 locations, then the second pair of lids can be placed in any other locations chosen by the students.)
6. One of the sealed lids should be placed alongside each of the open lids.
7. Students remove and examine the lids after at least 24 hours of exposure.

Suggested critical thinking questions

1. Explain why the four lids were sealed in zip-lock bags and placed next to open lids at each location.
2. Predict what will happen to each lid at each location. Was your prediction correct? Why or why not?
3. How does the hand lens help with your identification of the type and amount of airborne particles found at each site?
4. What are the likely sources for any particles found?
5. What devices might be designed to prevent the particle pollution that you identified?

What is the effect of pollutants on groundwater?

Background

Groundwater comes from rainfall that seeps *(percolates)* into *sediment* or rock layers that allow water to move through them. Many people drink groundwater. In many places, this water flows into rivers, lakes, and *reservoirs.*

Rainfall may be contaminated with acids from atmospheric gases. Rainwater also will carry surface *pollutants* into the groundwater. Such pollutants include *fertilizers, pesticides,* sewage treatment wastes, and chemicals.

Many people think that all of these pollutants are naturally filtered out of groundwater. Such wishful thinking may continue to encourage improper disposal of waste products.

Figure 13-3 shows a sand filtration setup for filtering pollutants out of water.

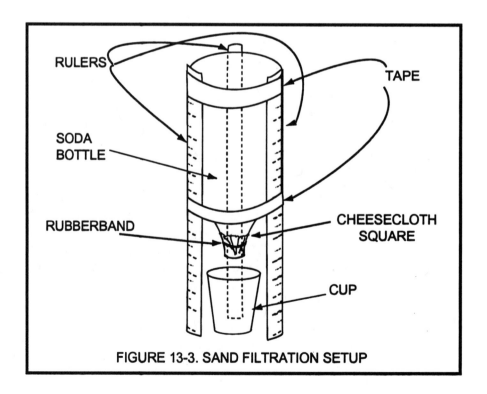

FIGURE 13-3. SAND FILTRATION SETUP

Materials

Per group of 4 students:

1-liter soda bottle
½ cup of potting soil
1 cup of fish tank gravel
4 cups of play sand
8-oz. measuring cup
scissors
4 teaspoons of lemon juice (to simulate acid rain)
20 drops of yellow food coloring (to simulate chemical
    pollution)
three 12″ rulers
masking tape
4″ square of cheesecloth folded into a 1″ square
1 small rubber band
6 oz. clear plastic cup
acid–base indicator (red and blue litmus paper)

Getting started

1. Students cut the bottom from a 1-liter plastic soda bottle (at the top of the base cap).
2. Students place a folded square of cheesecloth over the spout of the bottle and attach it tightly with the rubber band.
3. Students tape rulers at equal distances around the bottle so that the ends of the rulers are flush with the open end of the bottle (Figure 13-3). The bottle should stand vertically.
4. Students carefully pour the 4 cups of play sand into the open bottle. Next they pour in the gravel. Finally, they pour in and smooth the potting soil.
5. Students place the 6-oz. clear plastic cup under the spout of the bottle.
6. Students add the lemon juice and food coloring to the water.
7. Students should use litmus paper or acid–base indicator to test the water for acidity.
8. Students pour the water mixture into the open end of the plastic bottle.
9. Students observe and record the color and acidity of water that collects in the 6-oz. cup.

Suggested critical thinking questions

1. Predict what will happen to the acidity and color of the water as it seeps through the soil, gravel, and sand layers. Was your prediction correct? Why or why not?
2. How might the acidity of the water coming out of your filter column be reduced? Explain?
3. How might the color (chemical pollution) of the water coming out of your filter column be reduced? Explain?
4. What measures can be taken to reduce the acid levels of rainfall?
5. What measures can be taken to reduce chemical pollution of groundwater?

chapter 14

Humans can improve the environment of spaceship earth

| # What makes our environment a nice place in which to live?

Background

Humans have physical needs (food, water, air, shelter, clothing), emotional needs (love, feeling of safety, support), and *aesthetic* needs (pleasant surroundings). When these needs are satisfied, we can be physically and mentally sound and can develop into happy and productive adults. Helping to keep our environment clean and beautiful helps to make life more pleasant.

Materials

> enough dry "garbage" (scraps of paper, crumpled newspaper, plastic bottles, empty cans, packages, and packing materials) to cover the play space and desks or work tables
> 1 radio or phonograph

Getting started

1. While the class is out of the room, the teacher spreads the "garbage" around the room and turns on the radio or tape player to a loud volume.
2. As students return to the room, the teacher acts merely as an observer and does not respond to students' questions. The teacher makes notes on their comments and activities with respect to the room environment.
3. After a short period of time, the teacher organizes the room cleanup if students have not begun to do so.
4. The teacher reads students' comments and her own observations back to the class as part of a discussion.

Suggested critical thinking questions

1. What were your feelings when you entered the room? Why did you feel this way?
2. What did you do or plan to do to "fix" the classroom?
3. Why is it better to have a clean and quiet classroom?

4. How would you feel about your neighborhood if there were garbage spread around or constant loud noises? What could be done about these conditions?

5. Why is it important to have a clean and quiet place to live and work?

What can be done with our throw-away materials?

Background

The United States is facing many materials crises that impact on the environment of spaceship earth. One crisis is that many of our resources, such as *fossil fuels* and *metal ores,* are not *renewable resources.* Others, such as forests and clean air and water, require a long time for renewal. Another crisis is that waste products are rapidly filling the available disposal sites or contaminating air, soil, and water. *Conservation* and *recycling* of materials can slow the use of nonrenewable resources and also reduce the volume of materials going to landfills. For example, newspapers can be recycled into other paper products and cardboard. Aluminum and glass can be remelted to produce new products. Some plastic containers can be reprocessed to form new products.

Figure 14-1 shows the use of collection bags for sorting.

FIGURE 14-1. COLLECTION BAGS FOR SORTING DRY MATERIALS FOR RECYCLING

Materials

For each student:

4 large, supermarket paper bags

Getting started

1. Students label collection bags as shown in Figure 14-1.
2. Students should predict how many bags of each material will be collected by the entire class by the end of one week. They should record their predictions.
3. At home, the students will sort dry recyclable materials (no food scraps) into the bags for seven days.
4. Students will record, in their notebooks, how many bags or half bags of each material they have collected.
5. When students report their results, the teacher constructs a class bar graph depicting the quantity (number of bags or half bags) of recyclable materials collected during the week.

Suggested critical thinking questions

1. What does the three-arrow symbol mean (right-hand side of Figure 14-1)?
2. What types of throw-away materials can be recycled?
3. How do the amounts of materials shown on the bar graph compare to your prediction? Why is there a difference between your prediction and the class results?
4. Suppose that each class in your school did a similar collection. How many bags of each material would the school collect for one week, one month, and one year?
5. How much space on your school playground or schoolyard would be taken up by the materials collected for one year?
6. What can be done with these throw-away materials so that they do not take up useful space? Which of your suggestions would result in less use of natural resources and improve environmental quality?

| *How can we help to save fossil fuels?*

Background

Natural gas, heating oil, and electricity are commonly used for home heating. Much of the electricity we use is generated by burning coal or natural gas. All of the fossil fuels took millions of years to form. Therefore, over human lifetimes, they are nonrenewable resources, and we must make every effort to conserve them.

Home heating and cooling use more energy than any other household activity. The use of proper amounts of insulation helps to reduce the amount of energy needed to heat or cool an apartment or house.

Figure 14-2 shows a way of measuring the effects of insulation.

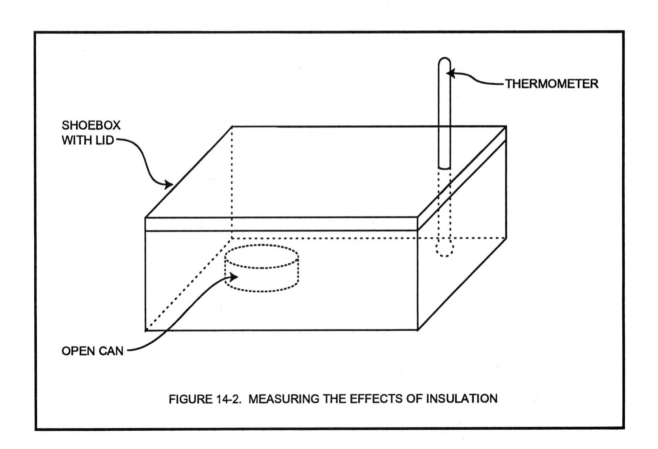

THERMOMETER

SHOEBOX WITH LID

OPEN CAN

FIGURE 14-2. MEASURING THE EFFECTS OF INSULATION

Materials

Per group of 4 students:

> 2 shoeboxes of the same size with lids
> 2 empty tuna fish or similar short cans
> 2 alcohol-filled thermometers
> 20 sheets of newspaper
> masking tape or cellophane tape
> container for pouring water
> very warm water to fill cans ¾ full

Getting started

1. Students rip or cut the 20 sheets of newspaper into two stacks of strips 3″ wide x 18″ long. Then they wrap and tape the stacks of strips around the outside of *one* shoebox. They will have to adjust the length and width of the strips for larger or smaller shoeboxes.
2. Students rip or cut the remaining newspaper into a 20-sheet stack, 6″ wide x 12″ long, and tape this stack onto the top of the shoebox lid. They adjust the length and the width for smaller or larger shoeboxes.
3. Students punch a hole for the thermometers near one end of each shoebox lid and insert both thermometers. The holes should be small enough to hold the thermometer in place (1″ below the top of the shoebox lid). Students tape the thermometers in place if necessary.
4. Students place each can in its shoebox at the opposite end from where the thermometer will be placed.
5. Students fill each can three-quarters full with the very warm water.
6. Students construct a data sheet that lists the time and temperature for each shoebox. Temperatures should be read every 2 minutes for a total of 20 minutes.
7. Students place the lid on both shoeboxes and record the initial temperature of each thermometer.

Suggested critical thinking questions

1. Predict whether the temperature in the shoeboxes will be the same or different during the activity. Explain your prediction.
2. Describe the effects, if any, that the insulation had on the temperature readings. Did this agree with your prediction? Why or why not?
3. Explain how you could change the activity so that the temperature difference in the two shoeboxes would be even greater. If you conduct this new experiment, do the results confirm your ideas? Why or why not?
4. What do you think the effect of the insulation would be if you tried to cool the air in the shoeboxes using ice water? If you conduct this new experiment, do the results confirm your ideas? Why or why not?
5. Explain how the use of insulation in heating and cooling of buildings contributes to the conservation of fossil fuels and the quality of the air that we breathe.

part three

Assessment

chapter 15

Using student experimentation for the authentic assessment of science skills, concepts, and attitudes

Definition of authentic assessment

Authentic assessment is a relatively new term that includes procedures known as "performance assessment" (Carey, 1994) and "practical assessment" (Carin, 1993). In their ideal form, authentic assessments would challenge students to meet the standards of performance needed for real-world occupations. Such standards include writing reports, conducting research, writing proposals, making models, assembling portfolios, and making presentations (Wiggins, 1989). Therefore, students would be engaged in tasks that they are likely to encounter as professionals, citizens, and consumers.

Authentic assessment of achievement evaluates student performance in terms of both process and product. It is this emphasis on performance that differentiates the authentic assessment protocol from conventional forms of assessment. The assessment should include a dialogue between "performer" and "evaluator" that provides clarification of questions for the performer and an opportunity for explanation of answers. An overview of types of performance assessment and examples of scoring procedures are given by Doran, Lawrenz, and Helgeson (1994).

Usually, conventional testing requires only that students recall and comprehend knowledge, whereas authentic assessment requires students to apply higher level cognitive skills, such as application, analysis, synthesis, and evaluation, to completion of the task. A comparison of the characteristics of conventional and authentic tests is given in Figure 15-1. It is obvious that authentic assessment is part of a more holistic approach to evaluation of learning.

Many classroom opportunities exist for employing authentic assessment procedures. The teaching and learning techniques described in Chapter 2 (experimentation, library research, field trips, survey research, debates, and model building) are all amenable to such testing. Our present discussion of authentic assessment, however, is limited to its use with student activities (experiments) that are performed as a whole-class evaluation procedure.

The activities in this book are best used for authentic assessment in student-centered, modified student-centered, and teacher-guided classrooms where higher level thinking skills are encouraged. In teacher-centered and modified teacher-centered classrooms, these activities probably would find use as teacher demonstrations or verification laboratories rather than as authentic assessment activities.

CONVENTIONAL ASSESSMENT	AUTHENTIC ASSESSMENT
Usually tests only knowledge and comprehension.	Evaluates higher cognitive levels (application, analysis, synthesis, and evaluation).
Emphasizes isolated facts.	Stresses interrelationship of concepts, skills, and attitudes.
Uses pencil-and-paper objective tests.	Uses observation, individualized discussion of process and product, and evaluation of student experiences.
Tests concepts and relationships not related to students' real-world experiences.	Tests concepts and relationships related to students' real-world experiences.

FIGURE 15-1.   COMPARISON OF THE CHARACTERISTICS OF CONVENTIONAL AND AUTHENTIC ASSESSMENTS

Activities can be used for diagnostic, formative, and summative evaluation. That is, authentic assessment of students' prior learning (including misconceptions) can be performed at the beginning of the school year using the previous grade's activities in this book. Then authentic assessment can be performed, during a unit of study, using grade-appropriate experiments. Alternatively, at the end of the unit of study, the activities in this book could be used for a summative evaluation.

Classroom management for authentic assessment of experimentation

The requirements and procedures for conducting authentic assessment of experimentation are the same regardless of whether it is done for diagnostic, formative, or summative purposes. In the following sections, it is assumed that more than one activity is being used for the authentic whole-class assessment session. Unfortunately, it is likely that, during the assessment session, time constraints will limit the discourse between teacher and student that is such a valuable aspect of authentic assessment.

151

Room setup (planning and preparation)

A teacher and/or teaching assistant will need to prepare the materials and equipment for the activities. The activities should be prepared well in advance in case problems arise in obtaining or checking the equipment.

The equipment and materials needed for the activities should be set out at stations. Each station should have the equipment for one activity. A label or card indicating the number or name of the activity should be placed at the station. The number of stations required will depend on the number of students participating in the assessment. Library tables can accommodate four different activities. When tables are not available, teachers should use some other form of large, flat surface. Individual student desks, especially small or slanted ones, are usable but not ideal. Each station should have a chair.

The size of the room required for the administration of the assessment will depend on the number of students participating. A science laboratory is *not* required for authentic assessment, but if the school has one, it is advisable to use it.

The stations

A *station* is a location in the room with the set of equipment and materials for performing an activity. Stations will be set up at different points around the room with an easy pattern for moving between them. Students will move from station to station, completing a set of tasks to which they are assigned. Only one student is permitted to work at a station at a time. It is important that both students and equipment can be accommodated comfortably so that students neither disturb nor help each other.

The equipment should be set out on the tables before the students enter the room. A sheet of instructions and questions pertinent to the specific activity should be affixed to the table at each station. One section of a station sheet may call for materials manipulation, another section may ask students to plan and conduct specific tasks, and a third section may ask the student for a conclusion or generalization.

In setting up stations, two crucial conditions must be met to create a valid testing environment:

1. No student should be in a position where he or she can easily observe an activity in progress that he or she may be conducting later. Activities should alternate around the room, and all students should be facing outward. Students should sit at chairs on the inside of the rectangular arrangement of stations.
2. The stations must be set up in such a way that when instructions are given (e.g., "Move to your next station"), all students will be able to proceed easily to the next assigned station.

For the testing session to run smoothly, it is important that all the students move at the same time in an orderly fashion. It is also important that students move to the correct station. For this to be achieved, all students must move to the *second* station on their left (or right). The same "directional" statement (e.g., move "left") must be given consistently.

In a typical 45-minute period, you may have time for only two or three activities per student. The schedule should include time for the activity, cleanup of the station, and movement to the next station. An alternative activity can be arranged for students who finish early at a particular station. However, most students should use most of the time allowed.

Some activities will allow equipment to be reused, but some materials, such as cups and vials, must be rinsed before being used again. Some expendable material will be discarded after each student's use and should be replaced from easily accessible stock within the room by the teacher or the assistant.

Prior to each testing session, the teacher and assistant should check each station to see if all the equipment and materials needed to complete the activity are present and to test the equipment. This is essential for valid and efficient test administration.

Instructions to the students (script)

As students enter the room, they should receive an answer booklet and be instructed to sit at a station. Generally, there is no prearrangement of students with their initial activity. When the students are seated, instruct them to look at the equipment in front of them and find their station sheet (sheet of instructions and questions).

When the students have settled in, the teacher may want to use the following script, which has been modified from Kanis, Doran, and Jacobson (1990).

> Good morning (afternoon). Today, we are going to perform some science activities. An instruction and question sheet, which explains the activity that you are about to do, is taped on the table at your station.
>
> Listen very carefully to the instructions, and do your best. Please write your name in the space provided on the front page of your answer booklet and fill in the other details. You will use this answer booklet for the entire testing session and then hand it in as you leave.
>
> [GIVE STUDENTS TIME TO DO THIS]
>
> This is a science practical test. The things that you will need have been set out for you at stations around the room. You will move from station to station until you have performed all the assigned activities. Carry the answer booklet with you as you move to the second station to your left (or right). Record the answers to the questions for each activity in your answer booklet.
>
> You will have ____ minutes to conduct each experiment with extra time in between to clean up and move from station to station. Do not begin any activity until I tell you to do so. Also, you must stop when I call time.
>
> Read the instructions and check to see that you have all the materials needed for your activity. Raise your hand if anything is missing.
>
> [PAUSE AND MAKE SURE THAT STUDENTS HAVE ALL THE MATERIALS NEEDED]
>
> Once you have started your activity, I cannot help you. I can only assist you right now if you have any materials missing. You will be given ____ minutes to conduct each experiment. After ____ minutes, I will inform you that you have ____ minutes left.
>
> We are now ready to begin the first activity. Are there any questions? Do your best. You may begin.
>
> [AFTER ____ MINUTES, MAKE THIS ANNOUNCEMENT]

You have ____ minutes to complete your activity before cleaning up your station.

[WHEN ____ MINUTES HAVE PASSED, GIVE THE
FOLLOWING INSTRUCTIONS]

Clean up your station for the next student. Make sure you leave the equipment as you found it. Do not move to the next station until I tell you to do so.

[GIVE STUDENTS TIME TO CLEAN UP. ALSO, MAKE
PREPARATIONS NECESSARY FOR THE NEXT
STUDENTS TO CONDUCT ACTIVITIES]

You may move now. It is essential that you go to your correct station. If you cannot find your next station, please raise your hand.

[GIVE THE STUDENTS TIME TO FIND THEIR
NEW STATIONS]

[HELP THOSE STUDENTS WHO INDICATE NEED]

You should turn to a new page in your booklet when beginning a different activity. Please write the number or name of the activity at the top of the page. You may begin work.

[AFTER ____ MINUTES GO BACK TO THE SCRIPT AND
REPEAT INSTRUCTIONS BEGINNING WITH
"AFTER ____ MINUTES, MAKE THIS ANNOUNCEMENT"]

[AFTER THE STUDENTS HAVE COMPLETED ALL OF THE
ACTIVITIES, GIVE THE FOLLOWING INSTRUCTIONS]

This is the end of the test. Please pass in your booklets. Thank you for being so attentive and cooperative during the test. Please wait for further instructions.

Scoring the test

This section on student evaluation by use of the Activity Evaluation Checklist (Figure 15-2) and scoring of test booklets includes some general guidelines and a review of the detailed scoring guide for one activity for a resource unit titled "Batteries and Bulbs."

Student evaluations in authentic assessments

Authentic assessment attempts to evaluate many aspects of the teaching and learning process. The assessments should be constructed so as to "point the student toward more sophisticated and effective ways to use knowledge" (Wiggins, 1989). In the school setting, we attempt to evaluate learners in terms of the affective, psychomotor, and cognitive domains as well as their demonstration of process skills. It is suggested that there are two stages in the authentic assessment of students who are using either the activities presented in this book or activities created by the teacher. One stage of evaluation is performed by the teacher during the testing period. This stage requires the use of the Activity Evaluation Checklist described next. The second stage requires the use of the individual student answer booklets, which will be discussed later in this chapter.

The activity evaluation checklist

The left-hand column of the Activity Evaluation Checklist, which follows, shows three major divisions defined by the affective, psychomotor, and cognitive domains and their subdomains. A further subdivision presents terms that identify student behaviors. We call such terms *descriptors*. Both evaluation of student behaviors and verbal discourse between teacher and student satisfy the fundamental requirements of authentic assessment.

As seen in the Checklist (Figure 15-2) the affective domain is divided into three subdomains: values, interests, and attitudes. These are further divided into descriptors, which give the criteria for evaluation. A similar subdivision applies to the psychomotor and cognitive domains. The Activity Evaluation Checklist detailing these domains has been modified and expanded from Trowbridge and Bybee (1993).

The Activity Evaluation Checklist may be used during the authentic assessment process and later as an aid to planning for individual student growth opportunities or for making adjustment in curricula, syllabi, or programs within one or more of the domains.

During observation of students performing authentic assessment tasks, the teacher will record the accomplishment or need for remediation demonstrated by each student for each descriptor contained in each subdomain. A scoring scheme could be as simple as using a + (for accomplishment) or – (for remediation needed) and no

Activity Evaluation Checklist

Class: _____   Date: _____

		Student Names					Interview Notes
Affective Domain Values	Cooperative, shares						
	Respects materials						
	Respects peers, accepts ideas of others						
	Neat and organized						
	Efficient in use of time						
Interest	Shows curiosity						
	Actively participates						
	Demonstrates enthusiasm						
Attitudes	Uses scientific approach						
	Uses scholarly approach						
Psychomotor Domain Manipulation of Equipment	Able to set up apparatus correctly						
	Dismantles and stores apparatus properly						
	Uses measuring instruments properly						
	Able to draw illustrations correctly						
Cognitive Domain Knowledge	Uses correct terminology						
	Able to recall and recognize						
	Recognizes symbols						
	Understands purpose of investigation						
	Observes phenomena						
	Identifies variables (and controls)						
Comprehension	Understands meaning of symbols						
	Able to classify						
	Understands diagrams						
	Measures and records						
Application	Can predict and hypothesize						
	Able to compare and contrast properties						
	Can graph and chart data						
Analysis	Able to interpret data						
	Can use inference						
	Applies problem solving procedure						
Synthesis and Evaluation	Forms judgments						
	Draws conclusions						
	Prepares laboratory reports						
	Contributes to verbal discourse						

Comments:

Sum					
Average					

FIGURE 15-2. ACTIVITY EVALUATION CHECKLIST

mark if it is not possible to make observations about specific descriptors. Scanning the marks in each column will allow the evaluation of the performance of individual students within all of the domains. This technique can lead to a plan for individualized remediation.

By scanning the marks in each row, the teacher can evaluate how well the entire class has done with respect to each descriptor. This leads to a rough evaluation of how well the class is attaining the stated goals and objectives of the curriculum, syllabus, or program. Or the evaluation may indicate that the curriculum, syllabus, or program lacks an emphasis with respect to some of the subdomains of the scale. In either case, it is important to make contemporaneous notes in the right-hand column of the chart about glaring problems or deficiencies with respect to specific descriptors. These notes will be a future guide for individualized instruction.

Rather than using only check marks, the scoring scheme could yield numerical data, for individuals or the class. To do this, values from 1 (low) to 5 (high) are used for each student with respect to each descriptor. For example, adding and averaging the scores in the column for each student will yield a numerical value for overall student performance. This may suggest the need for individualized remediation. Alternatively, adding and averaging the scores in each row will yield a numerical value for each descriptor. Such scores may be used in the same manner as was previously suggested for class evaluations.

A dialogue between individual students and the teacher is a requisite for ideal authentic assessment. However, given the constraints of authentic assessments with an entire class, it is necessary to modify the interview process. Therefore, individual student interviews are conducted on an as-needed basis. The purpose of the modified interview is to gather information from a random cross-section of the class. This may identify any misconceptions or faulty processing of information, which will then lead the teacher to devise plans for remediation. Highlights of the interviews should be recorded in the "Comments" section of the Activity Evaluation Chart.

The student answer booklet

The answer booklet contains written responses to the questions or instructions listed on each station sheet. The student answer booklet is important in whole-class authentic assessment efforts because it contains a record of the sequence of student thought processes that occurred during the activities. The teacher should analyze the content of these booklets in order to identify misconceptions and faulty thought processes. Such analysis may lead to follow-up interviews with selected students for further insights into their knowledge and thought processes as well as attitudinal and psychomotor difficulties. Results of the interviews may be used to plan for remediation of individual or class deficits within the domains. Or it may be that the deficits are the result of an inadequate emphasis in the curriculum, syllabus, or program.

Also, numerical grades can be derived from the authentic assessment of student investigations by scoring the responses in the students' answer booklets. An answer key is prepared which lists the scoring possibilities for fully correct, partially correct, or incorrect responses to each question. Analysis of the answers gives further insight into the knowledge and thought processes of each student.

An example of a station sheet and answer key for each section of the investigation follows. The number of points awarded to each correct or partially correct answer is arbitrary. This example of a station sheet and scoring key for student answers is taken from Kanis, Doran, and Jacobson (1990).

The example is an investigation that was part of a year-end, summative evaluation of fifth-grade students' knowledge of one topic in the physics curriculum. Other stations in the classroom contained investigations covering other aspects of the fifth-grade science curriculum.

Activity: Electrical tester

The following diagram (Figure 15-3) represents an electrical tester:

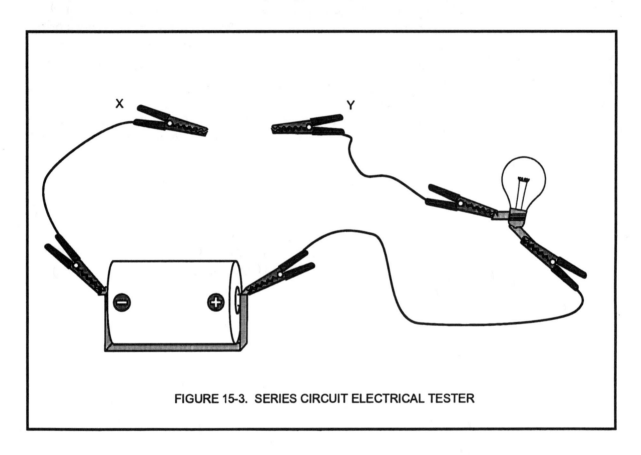

FIGURE 15-3. SERIES CIRCUIT ELECTRICAL TESTER

Use the materials provided to make such an electrical tester.

1. What happens when wires X and Y are connected? Check the appropriate box.

    ☐ The bulb lights.   ☐ The bulb does not light. (Please contact the teacher.)

2. Test the objects provided to see which ones conduct electricity. Place a check mark (✓) in the appropriate column to indicate the result.

Object	Bulb Lights	Bulb Does Not Light
Aluminum Foil		
Plastic Paper Clip		
Plastic Spoon		
Nail		

3. Which objects allowed the bulb to light? Give reasons for your answers.

_____

_____

_____

_____

Disconnect the wires when you are asked to clear your area.

Activity: Electrical Tester (6 points total)

Task: Determine if four objects are electrical conductors by testing in a battery–bulb circuit (Physics).

Step 1: Construct an electrical conductivity tester from a pictorial.

Answer	*Scoring*
A. The "bulb lights" box is checked. B. Any evidence of 3 successful observations in item 2.	2 points if "bulb lights" is checked and/or there is evidence of success with 3 objects in item 2. 1 point if only "bulb lights" is checked. 0 points if incorrect response or could not make bulb light. 2 points possible

---

Step 2: Test objects for conductivity, indicate results in appropriate columns.

Answer	*Scoring*
The following shows an example of a correctly completed table:	2 points if all four objects are correctly tested. 1 point if three objects are correctly tested. 0 points for 2 or less objects correctly tested. 2 points possible

Object	*Bulb Lights*	*Bulb Does Not Light*
Aluminum Foil	X	
Plastic Paper Clip		X
Plastic Spoon		X
Nail	X	

Step 3: Correct identification of conductors with explanation.

Answer	*Scoring*
The nail and foil are identified as conductors. **Explanation:** A conductor allows current to flow through it and reach the light bulb, causing the bulb to light. Other acceptable explanations: 1. Circuit is completed. 2. Electricity flows through.	2 points for correct identification and explanation. 1 point if only one part of the item is correct. 0 points for no object correctly identified or neither answer is correct. 2 points possible

---

If authentic assessments, using standardized investigations, are performed in a school district or state, then a summary of class results could be forwarded to the appropriate authorities. Their analysis would help in the revision of syllabi and programs. The proper use of authentic assessment by administrators and curriculum specialists is discussed by Kanis, Doran, and Jacobson (1990) and is the subject of the New York State *Pupil Evaluation Program Tests and Program Evaluation Tests: School Administrators Manual* (1989).

Writing authentic assessment activities

The general steps involved in preparing a performance assessment are presented in Finson and Beaver (1994). However, the text that follows presents more specific information for classroom teachers about how they can write their own activities for use as authentic assessment instruments. The procedure is adapted from Gott and Murphy (1987). A chart similar to the one presented on page 166 should be prepared as a worksheet to aid in the design of each authentic assessment activity.

Authentic assessment task worksheet

Class/Grade Level _____ Unit/Topic _____

Title/Number of Activity _____

Purpose	*Nature of the Task*	*Materials*	*Task Questions/Instructions*	*Scoring*

The initial labeling of the chart includes the class or grade level, identification of the unit or topic being assessed, and the name or number of the activity. Usually, a unit assessment will be *summative*. For example, a unit assessment on the "Human Body" may include topics such as cells, tissues, organs, and organ systems. However, *formative* assessments of topics included in the unit can be administered while the unit of study is progressing.

The name of the activity might be the same as the one on the station sheet. In this case, it is important that the name not hint at the concept being tested. For example, the "Electrical Tester" title used in the sample station sheet model avoided the use of the terms *series circuit* or *conductivity*, which would give away terminology needed by students for a complete written response.

The columns of the Authentic Assessment Task Worksheet are labeled to reflect the important sequence of developing the activity: "Purpose," "Nature of the Task," "Materials," "Task Questions/Instructions," and "Scoring." The category "Purpose" is completed by identifying which behaviors are to be assessed. Such behaviors include those related to higher level cognitive skills given by Bloom (1954). For example, when the investigation seeks to have students demonstrate their ability to "analyze," then the behaviors listed in the "Purpose" column might be "compare" and "contrast," which are components of "analysis." Or if some aspect of the cognitive skill "application" is being assessed, then we might ask students to "construct" a device that shows how an insulation can be used to keep a liquid cold.

The second column, "Nature of the Task," is completed by listing the format of the investigation: manipulation or writing and the process skill(s) that the student will demonstrate during the investigation.

The third column, "Materials," is completed by listing the materials and equipment needed to complete the investigation.

The fourth column, "Task Questions/Instructions," is completed by writing items that will cause students to initiate an action. These items will direct the student through the investigation. A single question may be used instead to initiate a series of activities designed by the student, which then lead to the answer to the initiating question. For example, if the question item is, "Which chocolate chip cookie is the best?," then the student will decide which criterion or criteria must be satisfied in order to answer the question. This will require the student to design one or more investigations to address the criteria: taste, size, weight, number of chocolate chips, rate of disintegration when "dunked" in milk, and cost per unit.

The fifth column, "Scoring," is completed by indicating whether the checklist, a specific answer key, or both will be used to judge the level of student performance. If a key is to be used, the items of the answer key will be written in the column and will include scoring criteria for full, partial, or no credit for student performance.

A completed Authentic Assessment Task Worksheet follows for the "Electrical Tester" activity discussed previously.

AUTHENTIC ASSESSMENT TASK WORKSHEET

Grade: 5   **Unit:** Batteries and Bulbs   **Name:** Electrical Tester

Purpose	Nature of the Task	Materials	Task Questions/ Instructions for Students
1. Constructing a series circuit	*Writing* 1. Charting 2. Recording 3. Analyzing data	"D" size battery Battery holder Flashlight bulb Bulb holder Insulated wires (6' long) & clips	1. Use the materials provided to make an electric tester.
2. Categorizing conductivity materials	*Manipulating* 1. Assembling simple series circuit from a pictorial 2. Designing and conducting a conductivity test procedure	Aluminum foil Nail Plastic spoon Plastic paper clip	2. What happens when wires X and Y are connected? 3. Test the objects provided to see which conduct electricity. Place a mark in the appropriate column.

Scoring/Answer Key

Step 1: Construct an electrical conductivity tester from a pictorial.

Answer	Scoring
A. The "bulb lights" box is checked. B. Any evidence of 3 successful observations in item 2.	2 points if "bulb lights" is checked and/or there is evidence of success with 3 objects in item 2. 1 point if only "bulb lights" is checked. 0 points if incorrect response or could not make bulb light. 2 points possible

Step 2: Test objects for conductivity, indicate results in appropriate
Step 3: columns.

Answer	Scoring
The following is an example of a correctly completed table:	2 points if all 4 objects are correctly tested. 1 point if 3 objects are correctly tested. 0 points for 2 or fewer objects correctly tested. 2 points possible

Object	Bulb Lights	Bulb Does Not Light
Aluminum foil	X	
Plastic paper clip		X
Plastic spoon		X
Nail	X	

Step 3: Correct identification of conductors with explanation.

Answer	Scoring
The nail and foil are identified as conductors. **Explanation:** A conductor allows current to flow through it and reach the light bulb, causing the bulb to light. Other acceptable explanations: 1. Circuit is completed. 2. Electricity flows through.	2 points for correct identification and explanation. 1 point if only one part of the item is correct. 0 points for no item correctly identified or no part of answer is correct. 2 points possible

Adapting existing activities

The activities contained in this book are not written in the exact authentic assessment framework discussed here. They were intended to be used with students who are exploring new earth science concepts rather than to be used in an authentic assessment procedure. However, the elements of the authentic assessment framework are present in each activity. That is, the grade level and unit/topic and title of the investigation are given at the beginning of the activity. The "Background" section contains the concepts that apply to the activity (first column of the Task Worksheet). A diagram and procedure ("Getting Started") indicate the nature of the task and imply the process skills that could be assessed (second column of the Task Worksheet). Materials listed in each activity are the same as would be found in the third column of the worksheet. Both "Getting Started" and the "Suggested Critical Thinking Questions" for each activity contain the information on task questions/instructions to the students that would be found in the fourth column of the worksheet. The "Suggested Critical Thinking Questions" of each Activity could be the basis for the scoring/answer key of column 5 of the framework, or the checklist included in this chapter could be used to establish scoring criteria for the activity.

Extending authentic assessment procedures

In this chapter the emphasis has been on authentic assessment using activities (experiments) in a whole-class setting. This is only one aspect of authentic assessment. A more inclusive authentic assessment would add evidence of student achievement contained in portfolios, written proposals or reports, completed models, and presentations. Such evaluations would require the same types of teacher behavior (observation, interview, and review of student product) needed in the whole-class assessment discussed in this chapter. It is simply a matter of transferring such teacher behaviors to the other types of student achievement that are amenable to authentic assessment procedures.

The activity evaluation checklist (Figure 15-2) is a useful tool for an ongoing authentic assessment of individual students. A checklist would be prepared for each student and would be modified so that the columns represented stages of conceptualization of a project as represented by additions to a portfolio, stages in model building, drafts of proposals or reports, and preparation for presentations. Herein lies the true potential for individualizing authentic assessment procedures.

part four

Teacher Support

References

American Association for the Advancement of Science. (1993). *Benchmarks for scientific literacy: Project 2061.* New York: Oxford University Press.

American Geological Institute. (1964). *Earth science curriculum project.* Boulder: University of Colorado.

Barr, B. B. (1994). Research on problem solving: Elementary school. In D. L. Gabel (Ed.), *Handbook of research on science teaching and learning* (pp. 237–247). New York: Macmillan.

Bloom, B. (1985). *Taxonomy of educational objectives.* New York: Longman.

Carey, L. M. (1994). *Measuring and evaluating school learning,* 2nd ed. Boston: Allyn and Bacon.

Carin, A. A. (1993). *Teaching science through discovery,* 7th ed. Columbus, OH: Merrill.

Doran, R. L., Lawrenz, F., & Helgeson, S. (1994). Research on assessment in science. In D. L. Gabel (Ed.), *Handbook of research on science teaching and learning* (pp. 388–442). New York: Macmillan.

Finson, K., & Beaver, J. (1994). Performance assessment: Getting started. *Science Scope, 18*(1), 44–49.

Gott, R., & Murphy, P. (1987). *Assessing investigations at age 13 and 15.* Science Report for Teachers: 9. Belfast, Northern Ireland: Assessment of Performance Unit, Department of Education and Science.

Johnson, D., & Johnson, R. (1986). *Circles of learning.* Edina, MN: Interaction.

Johnson, D., & Johnson, R. (1987). How can we put cooperative learning into practice? *Science Teacher, 54*(9), 46–50.

Kanis, I. B. (1990). Improving the elementary science curriculum—Science education for the twenty-first century. *The Science Teachers Bulletin, 8*(2), 23–36.

Kanis, I. B., Doran, R. L., & Jacobson, W. J. (1990). *Assessing science laboratory skills at the elementary and middle/junior high levels: Second IEA science study.* Monograph. New York: Teachers College, Columbia University.

New York City Board of Education. (1989). *Essential learning outcomes—Science.* New York: Office of Program and Curriculum Development.

New York State Education Department. (1994). *Frameworks for mathematics, science and technology.* Albany: Bureau of Science Education.

New York State Education Department. (1989). *Pupil Evaluation Program Tests and Program Evaluation Tests: School administrators' manual.* Albany: Bureau of Elementary and Secondary Testing Programs.

New York State Education Department. (1984). *New York State Elementary Science Syllabus.* Albany: Bureau of Science Education.

Trowbridge, L., & Bybee, R. (1993). *Becoming a secondary school science teacher,* 4th ed. Columbus, OH: Merrill.

Wiggins, G. (1989, May). A true test: Toward more authentic and equitable assessment. *Phi Delta Kappan,* pp. 703–713.

Functional glossary

A **acid**   a substance that turns blue litmus paper red and that can dissolve some earth
materials

aesthetics   the study of art and beauty

allergies   negative reactions of animals to specific natural or artificial materials in
the environment

amplitude   vertical distance between the top or bottom of a wave and the midline
of the wave form

anemometer   any device for measuring the speed of the wind

anticline   an upward bend in rock layers

atmosphere   the layer of gases that surrounds a planet

axis   a line about which an object rotates

B **barometer**   any device for measuring air pressure. Aneroid barometers use a sealed
metal container that expands or contracts when air pressure changes. Mercurial
barometers use a column of mercury that rises or falls with changes in air pressure.

basin   a relatively large depression in the earth's surface. A basin may contain a
lake, sea, or ocean.

bottom current   a flow of relatively dense water at or near the bottom of a lake,
sea, or ocean

C **calcium carbonate**   a chemical compound that is easily dissolved by acids to yield
carbon dioxide and water

calibration   the procedure for relating the reading on an instrument to a reference
standard. *Verb:* **calibrate.**

caverns   large underground openings resulting from the dissolving of calcium
carbonate rock layers

chalk   sedimentary rock (usually white) composed primarily of marine animals
that have shells of calcium carbonate

chemical weathering   the breakdown of rock by natural acids

clay   a type of sediment resulting from the chemical weathering of certain rock
minerals (feldspars)

condensation   the process by which gases change into liquids. *Verb:* **condense.**

conservation   the act of saving or protecting from loss or waste

crust   the solid upper portion of the earth's lithosphere

current   a large stream of lake, sea, or ocean water moving continuously in about
the same path.

D

deep current   a flow of relatively dense water at or near the bottom level of a lake, sea, or ocean

density   the relative amount of matter in a given volume

deposition process   the accumulation of earth materials that have been transported by one or more of the erosion processes. *Verb:* **deposit.**

dinosaur   any of the large group of extinct reptile-like creatures that dominated animal life during the Mesozoic Era of the earth's history

dune   a streamlined accumulation of sand that has been moved by the wind

E

earth   the third planet from the sun in the solar system

earthquake   the vibration of the earth caused by the rapid release of stress in rocks of the lithosphere and mantle

earthquake waves   rhythmic disturbances of the surface layer or deeper layers of the earth

elevation   height of the land above mean sea level

ellipse   a slightly or greatly flattened circle

emissions   gases or particles released into the air from natural or human processes

epicenter   the central area on the earth's surface that is directly above the point of origin (focus) of an earthquake

erosion   the wearing away and removal of the earth's surface materials. *Verb:* **erode.**

evaporation   change in a substance from a liquid phase to a gas phase. *Verb:* **evaporate.**

extinction   the permanent disappearance from the earth of any group of animals or plants. *Adjective:* **extinct.**

F

fault   a break in rock layers where the two sides of the broken rock have moved relative to each other

fertilizer   any of a variety of chemical compounds used to aid crop production

fold   a bend in rock layers that may be upward, downward, or sideways

fossil   the remains of an extinct plant or animal that are found in rock layers or in a special preserving medium like amber

fossil fuel   gas, oil, and coal formed from decomposition of ancient organisms

G

geologist   a scientist who studies earth materials and processes

glacial ice   the dense, semisolid material that forms by the compaction of falling snow over many years

glacier   a mass of ice that covers a large area of a continent (ice cap) or a mountain valley (valley glacier) and that may flow

gravel   broken rock fragments that range from pea size to fist size

gravity   the force that attracts all bodies in the universe to each other

gravity fault   a break in rock layers where one side of the broken rock has moved up or down relative to the other side

groundwater   the rainfall that accumulates in soil, rock cracks, and connected rock pores

H

hemisphere   half of the earth's sphere. The Northern Hemisphere lies between the Equator and the North Pole. The Southern Hemisphere lies between the Equator and the South Pole.

high-pressure area   an area of the earth where atmospheric pressure is greater than normal sea-level pressure

hill   an isolated, rounded, low rise in the land surface

humidity   the amount of invisible moisture (water) that is mixed with the air

humus   a surface layer of decaying plant and animal matter

I

ice cap   a mass of glacial ice that covers a large part of a continent near a polar region

imprint   the impression in sediment left by a footprint, leaf, bone, or other object

L

lake   a relatively large, enclosed body of fresh or salt water located on a continent

lateral fault   a break in rock layers where one side of the broken rock has moved sideways relative to the other side

lava extrusion   surface flow or eruption of molten rock (magma) from the earth's lower lithosphere or upper mantle

limestone   a sedimentary rock made of calcium carbonate grains and shell fragments

liquefaction   the process that causes a loss of bearing capacity in moist, loose sediment that is shaken by earthquake waves

lithosphere   the top rock layer of the earth's layered structure. It is composed of crust and upper mantle.

low-pressure area   an area of the earth where atmospheric pressure is less than normal sea-level pressure

lunar eclipse   darkening of the moon caused by the earth's shadow

M

mantle   a thick layer of semimolten rock material that lies below the earth's crust and above its outer core

marble   a metamorphic rock made of crystallized calcium carbonate

Mercalli Scale   a numerical rating of earthquake strength based on the shaking of humans and damage to structures

metal ores   rock materials from which metals can be extracted

meteorite   a large rock or nickel-iron object that enters the earth's atmosphere from space

mid-ocean ridge   a continuous mountain chain present in all ocean basins. It runs along the center of the North and South Atlantic oceans, but in the Pacific Ocean it is closer to the North American and South American continents.

minerals   any of the naturally occurring, inorganic components of rocks

month   the time period from one full moon to the next (29 days, 12 hours, and 44 minutes)

moon   a natural satellite of a planet

mountain   an isolated, irregular, steep rise in the land surface

N

natural satellite   any planet that orbits a sun, or a moon that orbits a planet

north geographic pole   the point on the earth, in the Northern Hemisphere, where its imaginary axis of rotation would penetrate the surface

O

ocean   a body of salty water larger than a lake or a sea

orbit   the line or plane that marks the path of motion of a satellite

P

paleontologist   a scientist who studies extinct life forms

penumbra   the cone of semidarkness formed by the shadow of a satellite of a sun. The penumbra surrounds a cone of complete darkness called the umbra.

percolation   the movement of liquids through media (like sponges and sandstone rock layers) that have connected pore spaces. *Verb:* **percolate.**

pesticides   organic chemicals used to combat insect infestations

petrified wood   wood fiber that has been replaced by minerals carried by groundwater

plains   large, relatively flat or gently sloping land surfaces

planet   a large natural body that orbits a sun

plate tectonics   a theory that explains the behavior of individual portions of the earth's lithosphere

plateau   a large, raised, relatively flat land surface

Polaris   a star, in the constellation Ursa Minor (the Little Dipper), that is currently almost in line with the northern end of the earth's axis of rotation and therefore is called the North Star

pollen   the yellow powder blown from plant flowers

pollutants   natural or artificial compounds that affect the health of living things

psychrometer   a device that uses a wet bulb and a dry bulb thermometer to determine the relative humidity of air

R

rain gauge   any device that collects rainfall, the depth of which can be measured

recycling   act of reusing materials

relative humidity   the amount of moisture in the air relative to the maximum amount of moisture that could be held at a given temperature. Relative humidity is expressed as a percentage.

renewable resources   raw materials or natural substances that can be replaced or cleaned for reuse

reservoirs   accumulations of liquids in basins or in rocks that have connected pore spaces

river   the flow of water in a large channel or valley

rotation   the circular motion of an object on its axis

S

sand   sediment particles that are generally smaller than gravel and larger than silt particles (between $1/16$ mm and 2 mm)

satellite   any natural or constructed object that orbits around a celestial body

saturation   the condition that exists when air contains as much moisture as it can hold at a given temperature. An increase in air temperature will allow it to hold even more moisture. A decrease in temperature will reduce its moisture-holding capacity. *Verb:* **saturate.**

sediment   loose rock particles

sedimentary rock   a layer of rock particles cemented by calcium carbonate, iron oxide, or other minerals

seismogram   the paper tracing of ground vibrations from an earthquake recorded by a seismograph

seismograph   a device for detecting ground vibrations from an earthquake

seismologist   a scientist who studies the origin and characteristics of earthquakes

shoreline   the line between the land and a body of water (river, lake, sea, or ocean)

silt   a type of sediment resulting from the grinding of certain rock minerals (quartz) into a fine powder

slope   a land surface that is not horizontal

snout   the downhill end of a valley glacier

soil   a sequence of surface layers of sediment having different mineral and humus components

solar eclipse   darkening on earth caused by the moon's shadow

solar system   a sun (or suns) and all of the planets, asteroids, and comets that orbit it (them)

soot   airborne particles resulting from the burning of fossil fuels

south geographic pole   the point on the earth, in the Southern Hemisphere, where its imaginary axis of rotation would penetrate the surface

stream   the flow of water in a small channel

subduction   the downward motion of ocean lithosphere at trenches. Many trenches are found around the margin of the Pacific Ocean.

sun   a very large, self-luminous body

surface current   a flow of relatively dense water at or near the top level of a lake, sea, or ocean

syncline   a downward bend in rock layers

T

terminal moraine   the pile of sediment that accumulates at the snout (downhill end) of a glacier

thrust fault   a break in rock layers where one side of the broken rock pushes up and over the other side

tidal rise (tides)   the general increase in height of the water surface and land surface caused by the gravitational influence of the sun or moon

trench   a deep depression in the ocean floor that is found where ocean lithosphere is being subducted under continental lithosphere

tsunami   a seismic sea wave caused by an earthquake disturbance of ocean or near-ocean lithosphere

U

umbra   the cone of complete darkness formed by the shadow of a satellite of a sun. The umbra lies within a larger cone of semidarkness called the *penumbra*.

V

valley   a relatively long, troughlike depression that may contain a river or glacier

valley glaciers   streams of ice that flow from the tops of snow-clad mountains

volcano   a mountain made from the accumulation of solidified lava flows or the piling up of debris that has exploded from the lava vent

W

waning phase   the time between full moon and new moon during which less and less of the moon's disc is visible

waves   rhythmic disturbances of a water surface. Wave motion may be felt at depths that depend on the distance between the wave crests.

waxing phase   the time between new moon and full moon during which more and more of the moon's disc is visible

wind   horizontal motion of the atmosphere

wind vane   any device for indicating the direction from which the wind is blowing

Other resources

Selected science periodicals

National Wildlife
National Wildlife Federation
1400 16th Street, N.W., Washington, DC 20036

School Science and Mathematics
Central Association of Science and
    Mathematics Teachers
P.O. Box 48, Oak Park, IL 60305

Science Activities
Heldref Publications
1319 18th Street, N.W.
Washington, DC 20036-1802

Science and Children
National Science Teachers Association
1840 Wilson Boulevard
Arlington, VA 22201-3000

Science Education
John Wiley and Sons
605 Third Avenue, New York, NY 10016

Science News
1719 N Street, N.W.
Washington, DC 20036

The Science Teacher
National Science Teachers Association
1840 Wilson Boulevard
Arlington, VA 22201-3000

Selected environmental and science teacher organizations

American Association for the Advancement
    of Science
1515 Massachusetts Avenue, N.W.
Washington, DC 20005

Association for the Education of Teachers
    of Science
Dr. William Brown
Old Dominion University
Norfolk, VA 23508

National Association for Research in
    Science Teaching
University of Cincinnati
Cincinnati, OH 45221-0002

National Geographic Society
1145 17th Street, N.W.
Washington, DC 20036

National Science Teachers Association
1840 Wilson Boulevard
Arlington, VA 22201-3000

National Wildlife Federation
1400 Sixteenth Street, N.W.
Washington, DC 20036

Selected science supply houses

Carolina Biological Supply Company
2700 York Road
Burlington, NC 27215

Central Scientific Company
3300 CENCO Parkway
Franklin Park, IL 60131

Edmund Scientific Company
101 East Gloucester Pike
Barrington, NJ 08007

Fisher Scientific Company
4901 West Lemoyne Avenue
Chicago, IL 60651

Frey Scientific
905 Hickory Lane
Mansfield, OH 44905

NASCO
901 Janesville Avenue
Fort Atkinson, WI 53538

Sargent-Welch Scientific Company
7300 North Linder Avenue
Skokie, IL 60076-8026

Ward's Natural Science Establishment, Inc.
P.O. Box 1712
Rochester, NY 14603

Index